Fay

Fay

In Her Own Words - A Living Legacy

GRACE LARSON

Fay

Copyright © 2020 by Grace Larson. All rights reserved.

No part of this publication may be reproduced, stored in a retrieval system or transmitted in any way by any means, electronic, mechanical, photocopy, recording or otherwise without the prior permission of the author except as provided by USA copyright law.

The opinions expressed by the author are not necessarily those of URLink Print and Media.

1603 Capitol Ave., Suite 310 Cheyenne, Wyoming USA 82001
1-888-980-6523 | admin@urlinkpublishing.com

URLink Print and Media is committed to excellence in the publishing industry.

Book design copyright © 2020 by URLink Print and Media. All rights reserved.

Published in the United States of America
ISBN 978-1-64753-153-9 (Paperback)
ISBN 978-1-64753-154-6 (Hardback)
ISBN 978-1-64753-155-3 (Digital)
11.12.19

INTRODUCTION BY GRACE LARSON

My aunt, Fay Poloson Haynes, was born January 4, 1926 in Helena, Montana. Fay's mother, Annie Mae DesChamps Poloson, was born in Indian Territory, Mansfield, Arkansas, February 8, 1889. Mae came west by train in 1910 and Homesteaded near Three Forks, Montana.

Fay's father, Dan Poloson, was born October 26, 1896 near Porumbacu, Romania. Dan immigrated to the United States in 1916. He was working for the Herron Sheep Ranch near Wolf Creek when he and Mae were married March 2, 1922.

They bought the Rattlesnake Gulch Ranch in 1929. Fay was 3 years old when they moved, by train, from Wolf Creek, Montana to the Lonepine-Niarada area ranch. The trip from where the train stopped at Perma to the ranch was 37 miles. They hauled all their belongings on old trucks.

Fay was almost 15 when I was born and 17 when my sister, Alice, was born. Fay was our Second Mom.

Rattlesnake Gulch was aptly named as Fay's story on these snakes will show. Fay went to school at Lonepine, Montana.

Aunt Fay was a woman of so many Talents. She could sew beautifully making most of her and Bill's shirts, dress coats, and dress slacks. Embroidery and, even crewel, were skills she developed. It took her almost 2 years to complete the Crewel of Bill on horseback. Fay's oil and pencil paintings are so well defined and will be shown throughout this book. She could make "melt in your mouth" pie crust too.

Fay knew good horses and rode many of them. Her very favorite was Night and next was Jule Bar. Jule Bar and his son, Jumpy Jule took Fay all the way to the Montana Cowboy Hall Of Fame. She won so many Barrel Racing, Pole Bending, and Western Show events over the years. She performed at the Calgary Stampede, Walla Walla, Grand Coulee, Washington, Lethbridge, Canada, and in most of Montana's rodeos.

Fay's rodeo life began when she was a teenager. She was chosen Rodeo Queen and held that title for several years at the Polson, Hot Springs, and Plains, Montana Rodeos.

She was Secretary for Jake Johnson's rodeo events for close to 10 years. Fay knew rodeo stock and met many good cowboys over the years.

The cowboy she fell in love with was working as a judge at the Polson Rodeo. He had a wrist injury, so he wasn't riding bulls, bareback horses, or bulldogging. Fay and he started talking and ended up married December 15, 1951.

They bought the Big Bend Ranch from Bud Lake and began their life of raising top quality horses and prize Angus cattle. Fay had a Palomino part Arab stallion, April's Diamond, then a Thoroughbred stallion, Riskulus. She and Bill bought Riftez, an Arab stallion, from a Remount Station in Nevada, then Jule Bar, a bay quarter horse, caught Bill' eye.

He was a son of Sugar Bars and a Grandson of Three Bars TB. Three Bars brought speed and athleticism turning blocky quarter horses into sleek built athletes. Jule Bar had all of these qualities; he took Fay to the winners circle plus his winning genes were carried on by his sons and daughters.

After Jule Bar's life was destroyed in the Missoula Fairgrounds fire in 1967, Fay and Bill bought the quarter horse stallion, Bar Blair; next was Triple Coen, and Jules Gold Bar. After Bill's death in 1975 Fay had 2 AQHA stallions, Lynx Little Cookie and Bard Parker. Bard Parker was an actual son of Three Bars!

Jule Bar's son, Jumpy Jule, continued carrying Fay to the winners' circle after his sire died.

FAY

Mae Deschamps Poloson

Dan Poloson

(L-R) Bill Haynes, Fay, Bert Poloson, Grace Poloson, Fred Poloson, Ann Poloson and Dan Poloson

Marie Poloson

FAY

Marylin Barnes, Jake Johnson, Fay Poloson

Fay Poloson Glacier Park 1948

Fay Poloson and Niece, Grace, 1941

Fay Poloson & Niece Alice 1944

Bill Haynes & Fay Poloson Wedding Day December 15, 1951

Fay on Jule Bar at their Big Bend Ranch

Haynes Ranch Prize Angus

Bill roping on Jule Bar Big Bend Ranch

Fay barrel racing on Jule Bar

"SINGULAR HORSEWOMAN FAY HAYNES" BY HELEN CLARK

How many modern women would drive 900 miles alone with a horse trailer and stallion behind a truck to run three barrels for three days? Five foot seven inch tall 135 pound dark-haired hazel-eyed Fay Haynes of Hot Springs would and does. Fay recently returned from the annual Spring Horse Show at Calgary where she split first and second in the final run, split second and third in the second go-round and placed third in the average. She has ridden her stallion, Jule Bar, to many championships. Spokane witnessed the pair winning a championship at its recent Inland Empire Quarter Horse Show where Fay and Jule Bar won the barrel racing and placed third in pole bending; Jule Bar was declared Champion Get of Sire and his daughter, Jule's Jewel, won reserve Senior Champion Mare. Jule Bar's famous daughter Jule's Lady Bar, a triple A winner, won the Montana Charlie Russell Futurity of 1964.

It was a happy day for Fay and husband Bill Haynes when they purchased to the then youthful Julie Bar from Quarter Horse raisers, Doug and Nancy Dear, of Simms. Today Jule Bar is nine years old. The Dears had acquired the horse as a yearling from breeder Bud Warren of Perry, Oklahoma. Jule Bar is by celebrated Sugar Bars and out of Juleo by Leo. There is a great speed on both sides of this family tree. The Haynes took Jule Bar to their spread near the foot of Whiskey Peak out from Whiskey Trail in the Valley of the Little Bitterroots in the Big Bend of western Montana. The ranch address of the Haynes, however, is simply Hot Springs. In this beautiful rolling country six miles from Flathead River, Jule Bar is lord of the domain and his harem of 15 beautiful registered Quarter Horse Mares. The Haynes also have 12 geldings and raise some part Belgian work horses.

Bill and Fay do not use machinery on their ranch. They believe in doing things the old style way, and they refuse to even have a tractor on their place. They even ride a saddle horse over a mile daily just to get the mail. One concession they do make: they contract their haying. But often it is necessary that one remain at home when rodeo or horse show breaks, and the one who goes in the one who stands the most chance of benefitting by it. In the last few years it has been Fay, for Jule Bar has put her into many championships. Bill no longer contests in the rougher aspects of rodeo — dogging, roping, saddle bronc and bareback riding and bull riding — all of which he excelled at in younger days and which he now misses, but more and more the ranch has claimed his supervision and attention. But they are a celebrated pair in the West, Bill and Fay Haynes, and in the horse world they have both won their decided niche in fame. Youth is still theirs, and their future is bright with promise as their Quarter Horses annually bring them new laurels.

STALLIONS

APRIL'S DIAMOND:
Palomino Horse Breeders Association #6915
American Remount Association # 23322
Foaled April of 1942. Dark, Golden Palomino

RISKULUS:
Thoroughbred Stallion, Chestnut, foaled in 1931. By age 5 he had won $31,540. In 2018 dollars this would be: $521,046.68

RIFTEZ: Arabian Horse Registry #4846 Sorrel foaled March 3, 1948. Bred by the U.S. Government. His sire, Witez II (the living legend), was foaled in Poland.

JULE BAR: AQHA # P-85496. Bay, foaled in 1956. Sire was Sugar Bars and Grandsire was Three Bars, the greatest speed sire of all time. Jule Bar and several of his offspring won many awards and AQHA racing championships.

TRIPLE COEN: AQHA # 738,646. Bay, foaled in 1970. He was double bred Three Bars. As a three year old he won 2 races, was a finalist in the All-American Futurity, and had earned 12 AQHA racing points.

BAR BLAIR: AQHA #225668 Chestnut, foaled in 1962. Grandson of Three Bars. Sired 14 foals. 4 of these from Jule Bar bred mares.

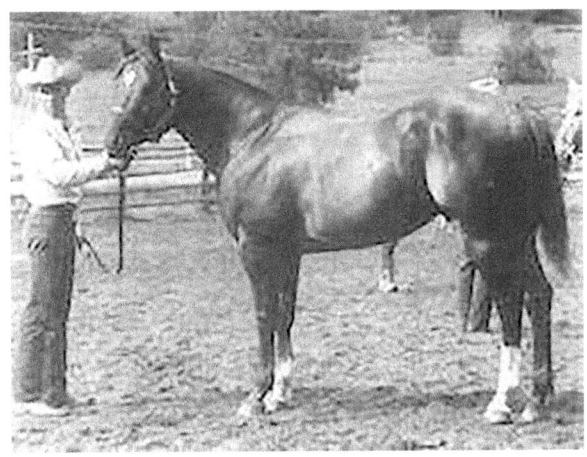

JULES GOLD BAR: AQHA # 406,829 Palomino, foaled in 1966. Sired by Hayne's Ranch stallion, Jule Bar. Joe Reed and Three Bars bloodlines. 7 listed offspring.

Jule's Gold Bar

LYNX LITTLE COOKIE: AQHA #2395346 Sorrel, foaled in 1985. Double bred Three Bars. 41 offspring with most a cross between a Jule Bar bred mare or a Bard Parker bred mare.

BARD PARKER: AQHA #0332843 Chestnut, foaled in 1960. 16 Hands and weighed 1350 lbs. Son of Three Bars by Percentage. Dam, Fay Parker by Chicaro Bill.

FAY'S STORIES

DAD

He gave everyone the benefit of the doubt, and he figured other peoples' word was good until they proved otherwise. Some took advantage of his trust, but he seldom ever said anything about it, just avoided dealing with them a second time, or at least was real careful when he did deal. He said, "Dey tink I'm just a dumb sheepherder but I'm not that dumb."

He liked horses. He could ride all day, day after day, and much of his riding was all done on a long trot. He covered more miles than one could imagine, yet his horses weren't played out or overly tired. He often would stop, sit for a while under a tree while his horse grazed. He nearly always let his saddle and pack horses loose. He said, "Oh, dey stay" and usually they did. He wasn't a great rider, and yet he could get along with some pretty spooky horses. He could hang more stuff on his saddle, and get by without spooking his horse, than anyone could. He trusted horses as he trusted people, and they sensed it. He had some good work horses, and some bad ones. For many years, he had a brown team called Dan & Prince, a faithful, honest pair of horses that did whatever was asked of them, and did it well. They were a quiet feed team. They could pull an outfit out of the mud with a steady, hard pull the towel either move the outfit or break the harness, or take the bumper off the vehicle! We used a lot of wood for the house, cookhouses & bunkhouses, and it was a work team's job to snake logs down for wood. Dan & Prince were tops at this. They would pull a log to the landing by themselves, turn off so the tongs would come loose, and wait for their driver to come drive them back up the draw for another log.

Dad had another team, Chief & Colonel. Chief was a big, beautiful black Percheron, and Colonel was even bigger, a Sorrel. They ran away a number of times, and there is not much that is spooked than a runaway team. They tore up a few wagons and harness in their day. Once they ran away from pulling up hay when the men were stacking loose hay in the pen. They headed for the barn and jumped the fence, one over the gate, the other over the fence by it, and the gate post between them. It upended them both, broke some harness, tore the post out, and Chief & Colonel headed for the barn. Their day's work was over. Dad liked Chief. He figured that horse could pull anything he was hitched to, and this was about right. Chief put his heart into everything, and although he got pretty excited and sometimes jumped into his work, when a real top working horse would ease into it, he generally got whatever he was hooked to moved. Once, a big log got away and rolled down behind the cookhouse. The other team couldn't pull it out, so Dad hooked Chief & Colonel, and when they laid into the harness, the log came. This gave Dad a chance to say, "I told you so," because he just knew that black horse could move heaven and earth!

Buddy was a favorite saddle horse of Dad's. He was a great big, tall, ungainly gray horse, kind and gentle, and he loved people. Dad used him for a number of years as a mountain horse when he trailed sheep into the St. Joe country on the Montana-Idaho border. Buddy learned the different campsites, and he could be sent on ahead to the next camp alone, and he would be waiting there when the rest of the horses and men arrived. Usually they would leave the truck or pickup at a certain place, and ride on into the next camp. When coming out, Dad could ride Buddy to the pickup, tie up his reins and send him back. The camp tender or sheepherder would unsaddle and turn him loose when he got there. He never failed. But one thing Buddy refused to do was load in the truck or pickup. Anything else, but not this. One time he was loaded, and he fought so hard and bruised himself so badly that they never tried him again. So he made the trip, spring & fall, from the ranch near Niarada to Idaho and back again.

He would follow the sheep, going back and forth behind them like a sheepdog. He would do the same without a rider. Buddy was a horse you could catch anywhere, anytime. He just liked to be with people.

Dad's driving would scare anybody. Ferris & Dad were in the pickup, coming down the steep ridge northeast of the ranch. Ferris said it was almost straight down where Dad wanted to go. It was fairly clear of rocks and trees, but mighty steep. Dad said, "It's okay, I rode a horse down here lots of times."

Bill Before Fay

Bill was born January 2, 1916. He came to Cutbank, Montana, from Pine City, MN, when he was 12 years old. Getting to Cutbank was tough as he and an older boy had hopped a freight train. When it stopped along the way someone gave them a ring of bologna and a loaf of bread. The train started up too soon; the older boy made it back on with the bread, but Bill dropped the ring of bologna as he ran and jumped onto the train.

Bill's uncle had a ranch near Cutbank. Bill was already working for a living wherever there was a job, and they'd take him in and feed him. He was a hard worker and liked to work.

1941-1942:

R.B. Leach's (Russell Byron) father owned a horse ranch near Dupuyer for years. Clark Gable's father, William Henry Gable, leased a wheat farm near Leach's ranch on Reservation Land. Gable dealt in oil, farming, and bought and sold horses.

Russell knew how a horse should be broke but never broke one; in fact he seldom ever rode a horse. He bought horses from Gable and others for Wolf Longman of Great Falls. Russell dealt in sheep too. He never owned any land at that time. He'd been given 3 hours to get off his Dad's place! He was a smart operator, never built a thing; anything built had to stay. He was mobile as far as camps, cooks, and the horses.

Russell hired riders to clear the stock from the fields; there were no fences. He made a deal to furnish Remount Horses to the government. He'd leased land from Bill Wilkinson, the sheriff of Pondera County. He bought horses from Montana, N. Wyoming, and Idaho.

The ranch was part of the old Frye Cattle Co.; it ran from the Sun River all the way to Canada, It had a huge barn with stalls for 24 horses. Corrals covered a couple of acres.

There was a high, stockade fence all around it. The round corrals and pens could hold several hundred head. Dupuyer Creek ran right past the buildings.

Bill Heil, Park Naughsinger, and Ira Clair Kimball bought horses for Russell. Usually, they were trucked from the Seller's to Ranch Headquarters. The government wanted 4 to 8 year olds, 15 hands tall or more. They liked horses 16 to 17 hands. Solid colors were preferred; no paints but once in a while they'd accept a Buckskin. The big, breedy geldings were cut out for the Officers. The large courser types were used to pull artillery. Soundness was an absolute requirement, and no gaited stock. Pace was not acceptable at all.

Inspection was done at halter. If the horse passed then he was saddled and ridden at a walk, trot, and gallop. Major Fudge was the main buyer. He was a Vet and Clerk for the Army. He ordered the rider to turn back at his command and kick the horse into a full run. If the horse bucked, but not too hard, he'd take it anyway. Too rough and he'd reject the gelding. These geldings were mainly Standardbred-Thoroughbred cross, big, stout horses.

The rider didn't dare skin the horse up or sore them in any way. If the horse was drawn up in the withers, Major Fudge would get suspicious. No spur marks or sore corners of the mouth. We couldn't fool Major Fudge.

Bill, and the other cowboys, continually rode horses; 80 to 100 a day, every kind there was from green broke to wild and broncy. Some were "good looking" and others had a Roman nose, poor withers, legs, and long backs. Those that passed were tagged for shipment; rejects were traded off for buckers. Roy King bought most of the broncs for his rodeos.

Paul Foote had 30 head of Morgans, 6 to 7 years old, and they were good buckers; some were spoiled saddle horses that liked to buck. Roy King bought most of them for rodeo stock. Bill rode some of the other Foote horses; all but 3 passed.

Bill never could get past a big Standardbred. He'd run away up and down the creek bottom, through the brush, and out into the open. There were lots of new trails along the creek bottom. Bill wore chaps all the time. He'd hang his slicker on the horn the first ride.

Bill never took the spurs off his boots. He'd show the big Standardbred but he was drawn up in the back and had scars in his mouth. Bill tried several times to show him perfectly but Major Fudge was skeptical.

Clair Kimball was Russell's foreman. Jim Hughes, a guy from the High Line, helped him with the business end. Others were Bronc Bartlett and Del Duncan. Russell hired one bronc rider who could turn a broncy horse into a doggy and gentle mount. He found out the man was chloroforming them. He wasn't a top hand yet he always asked for the toughest. He never rode one horse after the other, and the horses were not snubbed.

When he'd lead them into the corral they'd be bucking. When he led them out, they were quiet. Russell figured it out when the horse sneezed and cotton fell out of his nose! The guy was fired on the spot. Quirt, another cowboy, was fired too.

Quirt had shown a big, stocking-legged, 17 hand black to Major Fudge. He was bad to buck but did fine until the Major said "turn back." He popped the horse with his whip and was bucked off. Before he hit the ground, Russell had his checkbook out. Quirt couldn't even successfully show one horse to the Major!

Bill was promoted to foreman. He took this horse along with 80 head. He had 2 boys helping that winter. They kept some of the 4 year olds over until spring. The 50 head they worked all winter were spoiled or green broke. They rode every day; some days it was 20 below. If the weather was too bad they would ride in the barn.

Bill saddled the stocking legged black in the round corral. They had some horses in what they called "the hospital bunch." Russell pulled in and the first thing he asked was, "what is wrong with that horse?" Bill told him "what I'm hired for." Bill rode him around the corral; the big black never bucked, so Bill opened the gate and headed out. He rode up to the creek; no buck. This gelding was a Pacer. Russell told Bill he'd give him an extra $10 if he could keep him from gaiting. The horse was "herd sour" which excited him, and he'd break into gait. A woven wire fence was between him and the other horses. Big Black kept turning, trying to get back to his pals. Bill whipped him and he blew up; he took out the entire side of the fence. And he gaited!

No use taking him; they could get by with walk and trot, but he always started to pace. But when they showed the Remount Prospects the Major asked Bill to ride him by again, and he did pass.

Bill had a 15 hand brown broke, well reined, but he liked to buck, and he was good at it. He was gentle to mount from either side. Bill took him through the inspection riding at a walk. The Major said, "My kind of horse. I will just try him myself." Bill stepped off; the Major stepped on, placed his leg over the horn, relaxed, then dismounted. The brown passed.

The next was a blood bay called Slim, real breedy, pop-eyed, hound gutted. No buck until the saddle would slide back; then he would buck. Roy Williams was working with Bill. Slim gave Roy a lot of trouble but couldn't buck him off until the day the saddle turned; Roy ended up in the gravel bottom creek. Roy was so mad; he whipped Slim with his coiled rope. Slim never bucked again, but his conformation didn't pass the Remount inspection.

Leon was a big brown, real gentle to catch, saddle, and ride. Once he started to sweat he'd buck. Russell made a deal with Ralph Hoff, a horse dealer from Cutbank, to buy the Rejects. Bill and Roy Williams took Ralph to the horse pasture. Leon was saddled with saddlebags on the saddle. Ralph looked at Bill and said, "You ride him." Bill started to untack him, and he started to buck, saddlebags popping, Ralph decided he didn't want to see the rest of the horses if Leon was a gentle one.

They sold all of this bunch to Bill Welch. He sent his son, Jack, and a nephew from the Flat Coulee Reservation the north side. Jack was a good hand, not a bronc rider though.

He took Bill's advice when choosing saddle horses. Roy Williams chose Leon; Bill Welch said, "No," he's too gentle. 4 riders had started out; the horses wanted to run so they loped right along. They'd gone a couple of miles when Leon blew up; down came Roy. He tried Leon again with the same end. Roy said Bill could pick the next ones.

Bill was riding a big bay, Roman-Nosed reject. He was spoiled and had to be cheeked to step on, or he'd pull away and buck. He was so big and stout he could jerk a rider right over his head. Bill used trip ropes on him; this made a believer out of him; if a rope even touched his front leg, he stood still. He was too rough and snakey for the Army. Bill would ride him anytime he needed a big, stout horse. He finally traded for him so he'd have a powerful gelding to run horses on.

Russell hired lots of guys out of the bars. Some would last 1 horse, some 1 day. One boy acted like a good hand; he and Bill never rode together. One day Bill saw the boy's horse tied up; he went looking for the boy and found him sleeping in the hay mow. He'd gone to town, staying up late. His job was to keep the feed racks full for the horses and a team of black mares, and repair the corrals, etc.

The Sheriff's folks did not allow hunting. There were all kinds of game birds. Bill and Roy wrapped a 22 pistol in a coat and put it behind Roy's saddle. They spotted a Canadian goose in the creek. Roy had a shotgun in his car; he went after it, and shot the goose. The old man came barreling out of the house hopping mad. Roy gave him the goose for a dinner treat. A neighbor came looking for his pet goose. The old man said that was a pretty expensive dinner; a $5 goose. That was equivalent to $87 in 2019.

Roy was riding a 5-year-old Thoroughbred that liked to buck when a religious woman stopped by. Bill was just riding out and Roy was coming in. It was a hot day; she was all sweated up. She walked towards Bill, spooking his horse, talking religion all the way. Bill had a heck of a time getting away. "There's no use trying to convert any of us."

Roy's horse bolted past Bill, half running, half bucking. Roy's horse tried to jump the 6-foot stockade fence. He hit the top rail and just turned over, throwing Roy hard. Roy cussed, got up, and went after his rope. The religious woman was waiting to talk to Roy; him swearing & whipping his horse. He'd run the horse forth and back over the gate until there was no gate left. She finally stopped talking. Apparently thought there was no use.

Russell bought 3 horses from a guy near Valier; a spoiled horse and 2 four year olds. He sent word to Bill and Roy. They'd taken some time off and gone into Dupuyer for haircuts. They drew straws on who would ride and who would drive the car; Roy would drive the car. The barbershop was next to a bar; the Bartender was bragging up his wine and giving out samples. Bill and Roy hadn't eaten and ended up drunk. They went out to try out the horses; Roy eared the spoiled saddle horse and Bill climbed on. Roy turned the other 2 out. Bill's horse bucked into a yard fence and garden. He finally got squared away heading the horses out of town. Roy in the car; Bill on the horse.

The horses crossed a cattle guard and Bill's horse jumped it. Bill would have been scared to death if he hadn't been drunk. Russell never bothered them unless something important came up. He had 120 head of 4 year olds. They were halter-broke; it was March and they were to have them ready to show the Major by May 1st!

Some were a little thin from winter. They started graining 20 head. Training began with their hind leg tied up every time they saddled the horse. They'd ride the same way they were required to show the horse for inspection. Before they unsaddled, all the horse's feet were handled. Russell came by; "they are going good. Turn them out in the field and grain them." The troughs were under a big tree; each held 500 lbs. of grain. When the horses had enough the trough was pulled up on pulleys. Russell wanted them grained for a month. Bill and Roy said 10 days but Russell wouldn't listen. The horses were "full of oats" and worse than ever to ride. They managed to ride all of them once a week. Bill said they spoiled it for themselves; they had worked the horses so well. Russell thought it was the "real deal."

A guy from Lemmon, South Dakota was ranching near Dupuyer. He married a Canadian girl, did some rodeoing, and worked construction in Glacier Park, running a Jackhammer in the tunnels. He rodeoed weekends, at the closer rodeos. Some old easy bucking horse would buck us off; a ride twice as rank on the ranch was easy! We'd ride as many as 14 a day depending on how green they were. This guy was a pretty good hand when he was available. All we did was handle horses and ride.

Kids thought it was a good deal but some couldn't even saddle their first horse. Bill rode a Miles City Cogshell saddle; 14-inch swells, 15-inch seat, and 4-inch cantle. It weighed 45 lbs. He used "contest" stirrups and wore his boots out over the instep. He was on a "bug-eyed" gelding that bucked steady; him with a rock in his boot! Bill rode back to the buildings where he cut a hole in the boot and took the rock out.

Roy was on a big, nervous black. He was okay as long as nothing went wrong. Roy was riding him leading horses to turn out in the field. Bill opened the gate, Roy rode through; the horse spooked and jerked the rope under his tail. Bill said he could still see that horse go as high as the ceiling. Roy was bucked off; the horse ran away dragging the rope; he ran through the fence and was cut up pretty bad.

Bill stayed with Russell for 17 months. Roy left that summer for Calgary, Canada where he got married. Roy said he never wanted to see another bucking horse. Bill didn't either; one slip and a person's head would be kicked off.

Bill left for a while but came back, and was riding again. His first day, Russell had 50 head in a holding pasture. He hired a boy to keep the books on the horses ages, manners, etc. Bill rode 32 head the first day. Some were okay and some bucked bad. He rode them all outside too. The boy said he was a rider but he went off the side of his first horse. He got on again; he needed this job, so he'd ride that horse one way or another. But, he couldn't, he soon found out. He just wanted the job so bad. Bill liked him and told him he'd cut him easier horses if he'd stay. He did for a while. Russell liked him and put him to work on his wheat farm crew.

The last Remount horses in that part of the country were inspected at Browning in late Fall. Bill had the last Russell Beach horses. Bill had some moved to Bynam. Most needed riding; they'd been riding Russell's horses and neglecting their own. The stockyards were full of wet snow at night and yards deeper by day. They were wet and cold; the horses cold and humpy; even the gentle ones wanted to buck.

These horses were not pen raised and they usually weren't even halter broke until time to be ridden. People were their enemies and they fought mighty hard from fear, but some from orneriness. These horses were unlike the horses now days. 2 and 3 year olds wouldn't get to first base on some of their rides. No one had time to play with them; usually the broncs were used right from the start; as soon as we could herd them around outside. Once you got on some of these ornery cusses you wanted to stay on. If you got off they would jerk away and run off leaving you miles from home. On top of jerking away he would kick you in the belly as you stepped off. If you could hold on to the reins they would drag you all over the prairie as you tried to get back on.

Blood colts, about 950 lbs, were naturally ornery and bad buckers. A pinto Bill rode for Jim Hoffman was one bad horse. Jim didn't say 3 guys had tried to ride him and gave up. Old Bill knew and he had asked not to ride him. Bill saddled him in the alley and rode out; Old Bill following him. Bill rode along the creek; the pinto took off on a run, went a quarter mile and suddenly blew up. Bill landed with the saddle still between his legs. The cinch ring broke. Old Bill galloped up and chased the horse home. Bill tried him again and he ran away, not 20 feet from where he ran the last time. The pinto started bucking and got the best of Bill. Bill walked home while Old Bill chased him home again.

Bill rode him in the corral, in a big circle, until he was tired out. Bill hated to ride him and the only way was to tire him out. He finally got so he wouldn't buck but he couldn't be trusted. Jim Hoffman's wife told him to get rid of that horse. He took him to Great Falls where he got a big offer he refused! He should have sold him; a little while later both Jim and Pinto met death in the river. Jim could swim like a fish but he was tangled in the reins. His wet body kept the pinto from escaping. Jim had a bruise on his head; the horse must have kicked him.

A cowboy named Ralph told Bill there were some Army type horses for sale, cheap, near Babb. Ralph left with the car and horse trailer; Bill followed on horseback. All of Bill's clothes were in Ralph's car. Ralph never came back; 2 days later Bill found him, the car, and the trailer. Ralph was okay but the car and trailer were upside down in the muddy ditch. Bill's clothes were full of mud. They made their way to the Davis Hotel, Ralph on foot; Bill on horseback. Bill picked up the key to their room just as the heat brought out the awful smell of their dirty bodies. Tourists, holding their noses, turned away. With the trailer wrecked they decided against the cheap horses. The Army wasn't buying and salable horses had to be well trained for ranch work, and novice riders.

Loose hay was fed in 10-foot slabs. Rigs were loaded on calm days; 2 or 3 wagons and a couple of sleds. Bill said one person would pitch, the other would tramp it down before it blew away. They stayed even-tempered and good-natured even though the hay blew off as fast as they loaded it. "Now wouldn't a man be in a hell of a shape if he got mad?" The big round bales they have now last for years; they are the most suitable, and easy to roll out. Ordinary bales blow away. Bill said they had round bales stacked 15 feet high; they lost the load; down it came with bales rolling every where.

As I typed this, I was thinking that it was a miracle that Bill lived though all of these hard times, and was able to marry my Aunt Fay. They had 24 horse filled years together. Bill knew good horses. He picked Jule Bar, a horse that put their ranch on top with the best.

Bill and Fay traveled to the National Finals in Oklahoma, and to visit the National Cowboy Hall of Fame in 1972. They traveled to Oklahoma again to buy Triple Coen.

Bill rodeoed for several years riding bulls, bareback horses, and bulldogging. It is called Steer Wrestling now. After he and Fay married, he stopped riding bulls. Bill continued to ride bareback horses and steer wrestled. Bill started Team Roping and was good at it.

Then came Chariot Races: he had a pinto team and also raced Jumpy Jule and Jules Princess. He won several Trophies.

My best memory of my Uncle Bill Haynes is a rattlesnake story. We were riding about 5 miles east of the Poloson Ranch buildings. I was on a green broke bay mare. We had ridden into an area with lots of rattlesnakes; a den must have been nearby. I happened to see the biggest snake ever so I leaned back on my horse's rump for a better look. The snake rattled and the mare jumped forward. I tumbled off down her hind legs, and watched the snake crawl away! I still felt like I'd been bit! My imagination was in high gear. Bill caught my mare led her back to me, and waited until I was back in the saddle. Then he led the way as we continued on. Not one word of reprimand!

I knew nothing of my Uncle's background then; he was just my Aunt Fay's husband. Looking back now, I realize he was a Man of his time; a Real Cowboy. My Aunt's kind of guy.

Fay has been a widow for over 44 years. She said there was never anyone who could compete with Bill for her love. And I can sure see why. She could look forever and she'd never find a Cowboy like Bill Haynes.

Bill & Brownie

Bill & Cotton, his "dogging" horse

JULE BAR

Fay winning the barrel race
at Missoula 1966

Fay barrel racing on Jule
Bar Art by Elsa Jensen

Bill roping on Jule Bar

Jule Bar by Sugar Bars (Three Bars — Frontera Sugar) and out of Juleo, a double A mare by Leo, and out of Julie W (AA) by Joe Hancock, bred by Bud Warren, Perry, Oklahoma. We got him in the fall of 1958. (Foaled in 1956.)

He was never raced, but he worked any working event whether trained for it or not. He was a natural cow-horse. He barrel raced since 1961, was in the Top 6 in the MBRA every year. Was Champion AQHA pole bending horse in Montana several years, and

Fay pole bending on Jule
Bar Art by Elsa Jensen

runner-up in barrel racing several times. In 1964 he was undefeated in pole bending, open and registered. That was the year he was judged Grand Champion Working Horse at the Inland Empire Q.H. Show in Spokane, with points won in pole bending, barrel racing, reining and working cow-horse classes. In the fall of 1964, he won both the pole bending and barrel race at the Lower Snake River Valley Show in Boise, Idaho.

He has won or placed at many of the rodeos in the Northwest, and has won the Finals at Letherbridge 2 different times. He tied for first at Calgary twice also, and this year, in a field of 37 contestants, was second.

He broke a bone in a hind ankle in 1963 in an accident at home, but went on to win a 3rd in the MBRA standings that season. He began favoring his leg from then on however, and had difficulty turning the first barrel… it hurt him to jab his foot into the ground for the sharp turn. Yet he placed high in the standings even so.

In his lifetime he won approximately $9000 in horse shows and rodeos. Most of the time we traveled alone. He never was any trouble to haul or handle. We would go until we were tired; then I would find a good place to unload him, tie him to the trailer and feed him his grain while I rested, or ate lunch, shopped for groceries on the way home, etc. He has been seen in many a town tied to the trailer waiting to be on his way again. Last year, Shelley, our little Shetland Sheepdog, joined him as a travel companion.

I hauled him quite a lot with other barrel racer's horses, without any trouble… mares, geldings, or stallions. It was all the same to him. He was always interested and curious, but never any trouble.

Bill started team-roping on him this year, and when he latched onto anything he could turn back and pop a steer off his feet till he'd shake the ground when he hit. Jule Bar loved team roping. It was more interesting to him than barrel racing.

Pole Bending was a favorite game to him too. Right from the start, he took to pole bending, and in 2 years he never tipped over a pole, and won most of the contests. He wound through those poles just like a snake. And he could run! There was never any doubt about that. But he was always easy to control.

His colts have proved themselves at halter, working events and speed.

Every one that has been campaigned to any extent has been successful. His race winners include Jule's Lady Bar AAA, winner of the Montana and Charles M. Russell Futurities in 1964; Jule's Playgirl, A (unoffical); Whirlie Bar AA+; Little Julie Bar AA; Jule's Triple Bee; Jule's Bee Quick; King Jule Bar; Lady's Jule Bar; & Hepi Bar. He has had 11 starters.

His most famous daughter in the working and halter classes is Jule's Jewel, owned and shown by Con Johnson, Kremlin. Con's 4-H project since she was a weanling. Jewel has won and placed at many of the major shows in the Northwest. Another winner of the Johnson's is Jule's Taffy Bar, excelling at reining, Western Pleasure and halter classes.

Jule Bar's chores on the ranch were always whatever came before him. He could, and would, do whatever we asked of him and he asked no favors, no matter how hard the work. There is no use to say he wasn't favored or babied… he was. He had his own barn, part of the old original homestead log barn that no other horse entered. And he had his own stall in the horse barn and always the best of the hay and grain. Always in tip-top condition, he was never sick a day in his life, and he never looked better than he did last year. The only blemish he had was the slight puff on the hind ankle that was broken.

Jule Bar had so many cute little ways about him. One of them; he simply loved to follow the hay wagon or sled in the winter. As far as he could hear it, he would get real anxious to go to that sled or wagon, and if I started him on a lope he was very apt to kick his heels in play and run as hard as he could, slide to a stop behind it and steal a little hay off the back.

He was such a good-feeling horse, and many's the time he would jump the creek, kick his heels, and buck a little on our way to get the mail. Once in awhile he would get a little rough to ride, but he was real easy to pull up if the going got rough!

He loved life! He would back out of the trailer at home and run in the circles whinnying at the top of his lungs, letting everyone know he was home. And as he approached his old log barn, he would start to whinny and dance, so anxious to get in for the night. He would whinny at the creek or water tank when we took him to water, and at anything that pleased him… his grain or hay, or maybe just someone coming toward him.

He would carry anything on his back, and many a time we would have to carry Shelley when the cows chased her, when she was a puppy. He let me reach down and pull her up on him… often she would get to scared she'd jump up on his knee. The cats "roosted" on his back in the barn when the weather was cold.

Once, I got a late start for Great Falls. I was in such a hurry, and blew a back tire on the car, up the Blackfoot. It was on a narrow part of the road, and I unloaded Jule Bar, tied him halfway in a ditch, and jacked the car up to change the tire. We got to Great Falls finally, and got to the arena just as they called the Open Pole Bending event. There were 18 entries, and Jule Bar won. The reg. pole bending followed, and he won that, and turned around and won the reg. barrel race too. He had been hauled 250 miles and just unloaded 15 minutes before he contested.

Jule Bar liked to play games. He would carry sticks around, or stick out his tongue and wait for you to pinch it. He would walk around behind you, ears laid back, nipping at your back. When you turned around, he would open those great big eyes and look just as innocent as could be, just like he was saying, "Now, you know I wouldn't bite you!" He didn't know that, a lot of the time, I would watch our shadows, and so knew when he was close or when he was getting too close. He never did bite, but it was a game to see when you would catch him at his play.

He would run to the gate at night, anxious to get to the barn, and no matter how icey, muddy, or snowy the ground, he never slowed until he was right at the gate. Somehow he never lost his footing, no matter how slippery it was. Then he would grab the top of the gate in his teeth and bite down as hard as he could while he waited for you, and then he would nip at his halter. He always knew when it was okay to play, and when it wasn't. Bill never stood for this foolishness and he never did those things with him!

A BAD-GOOD HORSE

February 1967

Bill & Brownie

The American Quarter horse is noted for its good disposition and good, common sense, among other things. However on occasion one comes along that has an ornery streak, and Jordan Black was one of them. "Brownie" as he was called, was a tall, good-looking, dark brown gelding with a light nose of a mule, large, dark eyes that held a defiant and suspicious look, and the fine, arched neck of a Thoroughbred. He had a pretty star on his forehead, and white hind feet.

    Brownie was foaled in 1958 near Jordan, Montana, back in the open paradise country where there is still an abundance of range horses on some of the big ranches. His early history is spotty, but from what we gathered through rumors and correspondence, he had been fooled with a little and seemed to get the best of his would-be riders. This could have happened when he came to Washington or Idaho, or it could have happened earlier in eastern Montana. Whatever happened, Brownie never forgot it. He was a beautiful, intelligent-appearing horse, one that should have been able to learn anything and learn it in a hurry. Perhaps he learned bad habits as easily as good ones!

My husband and I went to a horse sale in Washington in the late fall, and were attracted to this handsome brown 3-year-old gelding. At the time, we expected to buy a second stallion, a young well bred colt to use on the ranch. We did buy one, and then when Brownie came through the ring both Bill and I immediately liked him. We surely didn't need another gelding at the time, but we bought him anyway, and headed home for that night, a 2-year-old stallion and Brownie in the trailer. Little did we know it, but we almost had a nightmare ahead of us, for the highways were solid ice for miles, and we could barely creep along until we got past the Montana line, headed east. It was one of the longest nights either of us had spent, but we arrived home in good shape and the next day looked our new horses over in the bright sunlight.

Brownie, we thought, was one of the best-looking colts we had seen in a good long while. He was real gentle, easily managed, and quiet acting. We decided this colt should get some special handling, that he had the makings of a top performance horse.

At the time we didn't realize what kind of a performance horse he would be! We had a friend who was training horses, and he put a very light rein on them, and seemed to do a good breaking job. We had so many colts to ride at the time, and so made a deal with this boy to ride Brownie for a month. A few days later we delivered him, along with a hundred-pound sack of oats to keep him in shape and reward him for deeds well done.

It wasn't long before reports began to circulate about that tough brown horse of Bill Haynes'. So we took a drive down to see what was going on. It seemed that all Brownie wanted to do was buck. He had a vile disposition and he would stall and sull, and he'd buck every chance he got. He was handling a little, and it appeared he had been fooled with before, since he reined a little from the start. He was being ridden everyday; some by the fellow who was supposed to train him, and some by a neighbor of his, who was a bucking horse rider. It seemed that Brownie had turned into quite a bucking horse!

So we paid his training bill and brought him home. Bill began to ride him, and so began a long period of hard work for both man and horse, what appeared to be a fight to the finish and nobody knew for a while which would win. Brownie was plain spoiled, and he wasn't going to be broke. I suggested the horse be sold as a canner, bucking horse, or anything else, as long as we got rid of him, feeling that the time Bill was putting into him was being completely wasted, and he could be working 2 or 3 good colts and getting desirable results rather than fooling with the brown. And he was dangerous, a treacherous, ornery rascal with never a kind thought in his head.

He would sull, buck backwards, act as though he was going to throw himself, and once he started bucking, he didn't quit until he was played out.

And Bill stayed with him. He said he would break him or kill him, that he had too much money in the horse to can him. However, I believe it was the challenge to break the horse that made him stay at the job. He always did love to fool with broncs anyway.

He would saddle up, ride the brown horse until he straightened out, and head him for the mountains. The pair would disappear for hours at a time, which caused no little concern with me, because Brownie had shown too many times his mean side, and in this steep, rough country, anything could happen. But Bill always came back on him, old Brownie with his head hanging, sweating all over, fading out more and more as the summer went on, from sweat and sunshine and hard work. But his spirit didn't fade, and often he would come home so tired it looked as though he could barely move, and at the barn door he would break in two and buck again.

Many times Bill ran horses on him, and it was the same thing; Brownie came home completely worn out, and while he was tied to the fence he would suddenly start to buck and (never tightening his bridle reins) he would buck in one spot, then stop with a big hump in his back and stand there, looking around and snorting.

Even standing in the barn (he had a fairly narrow stall in the back of the barn) every now and then we would hear a commotion, and there would be ol' Brownie, almost sticking to the saddle horn through the ceiling of the barn as he bucked at the end of his halter rope.

Locoed? Maybe so. We had never been around a really locoed horse, but someone informed us the horse acted as though he had been locoed at one time. Could be… we never knew.

We kept Brownie for nearly 5 years. He made many a hard mile during that time, and eventually became a real outstanding using horse. However, he had every opportunity to do so, and had he been cooperative his jobs would have been so much easier for all concerned.

We have a neighbor who always likes to try out a new horse. He is in his 80's now, still a good old cowman, and knew the story of Brownie, but didn't recognize him one day when we rode over to visit. We left Brownie and my saddle horse in the corral while we "coffeed-up" at the house. This old cowboy went to the corral ahead of us, and what did we see when we arrived, but Brownie standing all humped up, practically grown to the spot, and the old fellow on his back. Bill approached him as easily as possible and told him that was the brown horse that had been bucking so much. The old rancher got off in a hurry, came around and grinned and said very proudly, "Well, I rode him anyway!"

Gradually, Brownie quit bucking when Bill was riding him. He'd had a siege or two of the quirt, which seemed to be the only thing that would make him stop bucking. He learned to respect the quirt, or a rope, and it wasn't too long before Bill was doing a little roping on him. He was careful however, because anything set Brownie off.

He was working cattle, running horses, doing a little roping, and finally one day Bill decided to take him to a jackpot rodeo where they were trying out some bucking horses. And he used Brownie hazing stock from the arena, and then tried him picking up bucking horses. Brownie seemed to enjoy running into those bucking horses, and didn't even mind when the cowboys piled off on him. One boy got bucked off a big saddle-bronc, and just as Bill rode in to pick him up, he came down, feet first, right on Brownie's hips. The horse paid no attention at all.

As long as he was doing everything else, he may as well be a packhorse too, so a packhorse he was, and a good one. He scattered things a little at first, but Bill would snub him up close and take off on a trot, not giving him enough head to do much bucking. After he got through humping and crow hopping along, he was an excellent packhorse. He gradually became used to this new chore, and just a humped back was the only indication that he didn't care too much for it.

And then he became a team roping horse, and a good one. He would wait and watch for the steer to come out, squatted and ready, and he would put his rider up on a steer in fast time. He worked a good rope and was all business in this event, and apparently his orneriness was all behind him, finally. He would head or heel equally well.

And so the story goes of Jordan Black, the dark horse that became one of the most versatile horses we ever owned, but also one of the most difficult horses to break. Hard, steady work seemed to do the job, and about the time Bill decided to add another job to his list (he was going to make a chariot-racing horse of Brownie,) he sold him to a team roper on the east side of the mountains. Brownie had settled down to become a top using horse, a trusted horse that anyone could safely ride.

Perhaps he was one in a great many... a registered Quarter Horse with a bad disposition, difficult to break. Or somewhere along the line, was he spoiled, locoed, or what? What was the dim, dark secret in his mind that took so many years to fade? We will never know.

MOSS HORSES

Fay & Carl Moss

About 200 head of Moss Horses

At Rest

Like a page out of a Western history, the trailing of the Moss Ranch Quarter horses from near Charlo, Montana to the West Irving Flats country west of Polson, drew 14 riders from eastern Washington to travel along with the crew of local cowboys and cowgirls.

Well-known for many years, Carl and Kathy Moss have been recognized for their top quality horses, with the best of bloodlines, and raised up in high, rough country along the Flathead River, southwest of Ronan. In the drive were over 200 head of registered horses with close-up Three Bars, Top Deck, Joe Reed breeding.

After the sale of the Moss Ranch, Carl, Kathy, and their family leased pasture on Irving Flats, and it took 2 days to trail the horses to their new place. Carl, Shane, Travis, and Keela were all riding horses they raised. The trip was easy for them, partly because they had been ridden a lot lately, and partly due to the fact that the rough country they were raised in had hardened them physically and given them hoofs like iron and endurance for a long, hard trip, and a lot of running.

It was around 11 o'clock in the first morning that the drive got underway, with riders combing the hills to gather the horses and bring them down to the flats along the river. This was no easy task, with all the mares breaking for the mountains and freedom with every chance they got. The steep, rocky country was easy for them, since they had known the country since birth. But it taxed a flatland saddle horse that wasn't used to the rough country and the rocks.

And the horses were used to being chased, to the corrals, to a different pasture, and this to them was no different. They learned at an early age to run from horseback riders, and they learned well. They did respect fences however, and this was fortunate because they could be held along fence-lines to slow and quiet them. When they reached the flat country they started to mill, and many a mile was made just circling until they slowed down.

The first lap of the trip was soon over, as they approached Sloan's Bridge and went up to the Little Bitterroot River to the overnight spot. The horses were turned loose in a large pasture, and the riders unsaddled and took care of their horses. The Washington people camped out after a good supper taken care of by Kathy and her daughters, and friends who came to help. Horses were picketed or tied for the night.

The next morning saw trailers coming in, horses being readied, and riders headed out for the gather. A gate was left opened, and the horses had escaped to another pasture. However, it was no problem to gather them and head north along the Flathead River. This was a beautiful ride, mostly done at a lope to begin with, and gradually the horses slowed. By now they were used to being herded, and had lost most of their fear of riders.

After traveling along the foothills, through river breaks, and over the lower hills, the new pasture was reached, and a lot of tired horses and riders went home with some wonderful memories.

Probably the most influential sire, and the one Carl was most proud of, was Cats B Bar, a son of Birthday Bar by Three Bars, out of Catechue's Last by Catechu. Many of the Moss Ranch broodmares are by "Cats B" as well as granddaughters by the old horse. He had a speed index of 102, was a sorrel-roan with stockings and blaze.

Another horse that has left his mark on the herd is "Mac," the pretty little bay son of Sugar Bars, out of a Double Bid mare.

Jule's Gold Bar, by Jule Bar, Jet Smooth (2), Seattle Slew son, Buckaroo Bandit.

SHORT CUT

Art by Elsa Jensen

We won't use his real name. We'll just call him Bill. It was quite a few years ago that Bill hired out to break horses on one of the main ranches in the Cut Bank, Montana country, the Bill Welch Ranch. They ran a lot of cattle and horses at the time, and branded the Bar FT. The horses carried a lot of Thoroughbred breeding, most of them 3/4 and 7/8, and at that time, none of them, or at least very few, were broke under four years of age. They were ranged-raised horses, not like horses nowadays, and about the only time they ever saw a person was when they were gathered to be branded, or gelded, or when someone would chase them on a saddlehorse. They were wild from the word go, and it took a hand to break them.

Bill spent a lot of time with these horses through the years, and he rode a lot of good horses during that time. Most of them bucked, and they were laying for you all the time. He rode contest stirrups with his feet jammed in as far as they would go, to where he wore the insteps out of his boots. His saddle, a double rig outfit, had some swells but wasn't a real bad bronc saddle. But a low roping saddle would leak too bad on that kind of horse, when a fellow is riding miles from the ranch and his horse blows up, he just about has to stay with him or walk home.

He used a hackamore on all those horses to begin with, and at the start he used hobbles on them and often picketed them so they would learn to respect a rope. Some of the worst ones he used trip tropes on.

The Reclamation was handling the big canal that watered Seville Flats, and bill hired on to patrol the ditch, to watch for holes or breaks. This canal ran from Two Medicine Dam next to the mountains, for some 27 miles, winding through the country south of Browning toward Cut Bank. This job made some good long rides for the broncs, besides bringing in some extra cash. So Bill would have his broncs stationed here and there along the route, and he would change whenever he came to the next horse. The Irrigation Boss never knew who was riding if he saw him at a distance because he couldn't keep track of all the horses. He didn't like that either. He was at the head-quarters corrals everyday when Bill took off, to make sure he was on the job and had the necessary provisions. It was a rule that the riders must carry a shovel, so Bill got himself a little Army shovel with a scabbard, tied it onto his saddle along with his slicker and hobbles, and the also necessary gunny sacks. These sacks were to be filled with sand or dirt and dropped into holes to plug them.

The boss always said, "Is that a bronc?" for he didn't like the idea of his rider patrolling on some unruly horse. "Well," Bill would answer, "he was yesterday but he ain't today."

There were a lot of gophers in the country, and they would tunnel underground and sometimes cause a break in the irrigation canal. The water would keep eroding and enlarging the hole until it would become an underground tunnel and cause a major break in time. So the idea was to plug these holes and breaks as soon as possible to keep the water running down the ditch where it belonged. This particular day, Bill had lost his gunny sacks, so he was using an easier way to remedy the damage. He would simply ride his horse into the canal, turn him around and around and tramp the dirt and mud into the hole. This method worked too.

He got in a deep hole, and things began to happen. The horse he was riding this trip was a big, good-looking bay, about a 3/4 Thoroughbred, a little heavier built horse than the usual Bar FT stock. He was even a little feather-legged, maybe a little work-horse breeding away back someplace. He was a real snotty horse and spooky, and when he dropped into that hole he had a fit.

At this point, the canal ran toward main #2 highway. It made a big bend just between where the leak was located and the highway bridge that crossed the canal. It was probably about a quarter of a mile from the leak in the canal to the bridge.

When the bay bronc started to go under, Bill stepped off and landed on the bank. He had hold of the hackamore reins yet, but away out at the ends, and the horse jerked away from him. Rather than come back to the near bank, he swam across the canal and came out on the far bank. It was about thirty feet across the water at this point, and probably 10 or 12 feet deep. Well, the bay bronc scrambled up the bank and stood there looking back at Bill with his reins trailing.

Bill usually had these horses pretty well-trained to ground tie so he wasn't too concerned about losing this one.

Since it was about a half-mile walk to the bridge and back down the other side of the canal, and only a matter of a few feet across the canal at this point, Bill figured it would be a lot easier to just cross the water. Besides, by the time he walked clear around, the horse might decide to leave. Sometimes it's a good idea to try and do things the easy way and take a short cut, and sometimes it wasn't!

There hadn't been a car in sight for a long time, so Bill figured it was safe to swim across in his birthday suit, catch his horse and come back for his clothes. Which is just what he started out to do. But he had no sooner got across the canal when a car appeared out of nowhere, so he laid down by the bank to hide. The horse was watching him pretty suspicious-like, and snorting softly to himself.

Soon as the car got up the road a ways, Bill came out of hiding and went to catch his horse. The horse had other ideas. The man that had been riding with him was a heap different looking character than this washed-out looking creature approaching. He wouldn't run. He just kept backing up, circling, snorting and trailing his reins, keeping barely out of reach, and working toward the highway. To make matters worse, it seemed as though half of the next town was on the highway about this time, and Bill had to duck behind clumps of grass or mounds of dirt every so often.

And to help things along, the ground was still covered with those little cactus plants, and they sure are sharp on a bare foot. Bill hadn't walked barefooted in a long time, and he never did have any practice walking on cactus barefooted, so you can bet your life he was being mighty careful. He was busy watching the ground, the highway, and his horse, all at the same time.

The bay was so spooked that Bill didn't dare make any quick moves to grab the reins either. So far he was keeping his face towards the cowboy, trailing the reins and just sidestepping or backing to escape this fearful thing. He never did turn tail and Bill knew just one wrong move could set him off. Once he got turned away and started to run, he probably wouldn't stop till he got home. He was rolling his eyes, snorting, sticking out his nose, swinging around to keep the reins ahead of him, and dancing sideways. And just barely out of reach.

Finally Bill got a hold of the reins. Then there came another car! But at least he had the horse to duck behind this time. But no! The Horse had other ideas and tried to pull away. It was either hide and lose the horse, or hang onto the horse. Bill hung on. He managed to maneuver the horse around so it was between himself and the car, most of the time anyway.

Now, to get close enough to get on the cuss! This was no easy chore, but finally Bill coaxed until he got near enough to get on and ride, the pop-eyed, frightened horse back through the canal where he dressed and went on about his work.

So this was one time when a short-cut didn't work!

RATTLESNAKES

The ranch where I was raised as it looked back in the days I mention in this story.

This country was homesteaded in 1910, and there were sixteen families in this gulch at one time. There was an old log schoolhouse a mile west of home, and it stood until about 1952. There are deep holes all over the sagebrush flat, where wells were dug, or dug at. Of course the people who settled there had know way of knowing that 160 acres in this drylands country would be practically worthless.

My folks now have the only ranch left in the Gulch. (Incidentally, this gulch was called "Rattlesnake Gulch.") They raised sheep, cattle, and horses until recent years, when they turned to cattle alone.

Rattlesnake Gulch is located north of Hot Springs, Montana, in the northwestern part of the state, between the little towns of Lonepine and Niarada.

RATTLESNAKES

One of my earliest recollections is of my mother warning us four children to watch out for rattlesnakes. Oh yes, we learned about snakes at a very early age! I was raised where they were rattlesnakes and have killed many of them. As long as I can see them, they don't scare me much, but I do have a fear of them just the same.

We made our own entertainment on the ranch in those days. Horse-back riding was the main pastime of course, and often we rode from daylight until after dark.

What strange toys we had! I can remember picking up a big, long bullsnake by the tail. And not only that, but I can remember getting on my horse bareback, riding like a wild person with that big snake dangling down the horse's hips, taking the fastest ride he ever took in his life or since! Such nerve we had then. Today I have such a dread of touching even the most harmless water snake that I shudder to even think of it. So strong is my dislike for rattlesnakes that to touch a picture of one will give me chills. The sound of their rattle is almost impossible to describe, yet instinct tells a person what it is almost from the first time they hear it. A rattlesnake probably kills a lot of field mice and other rodents, but I believe I would just as soon find another way of ridding the country of such things.

I always hated to come onto rattlesnake and not be able to kill it. This often happens however, where there are holes or rocky areas, or even sometimes tall grass or brush. Sometimes it is best to let well enough alone than to hunt when you don't know where to look. And you might just step on the snake anytime.

A very bad thing is to crush rattles or cut them off, and let a snake go. Generally a snake will rattle a warning, and if his rattles are gone, then his last method of warning is gone, and so the safety measure for all other living things is gone.

Many's the time I have been walking or running in tall grass, through rocks or bushes, and heard that warning rattle. Luckily I never did get bit, and I always had a respect for snakes because it seemed to me that they did warn before striking. This isn't true in all cases however. I was walking along a hillside once on a rather chilly day in early April. It was too early for rattlesnakes to be out, or so I thought, and I was taking no precautions. Just as I passed a small rock (I wasn't watching the ground particularly at any time, and apparently this time I was looking elsewhere,) I heard a rattle. I knew it was a snake of course, but it was behind me. I looked back, and from where it lay to my path could not have been more than a foot. Maybe it didn't hear me pass and maybe it was cold and took that long for it to rattle. Whatever it was I don't know. I also don't know if it was ready to strike as I went by and didn't, simply because it felt that I was harmless, or if it didn't even know I was there until after I was already past.

I have killed rattlesnakes off a saddle-horse, in tall grass where I was afraid I'd step on another one if I should get off the horse. It has often been said that, where you see one snake you see another. I have not found this to be the rule, but just the same it isn't wise to take a chance.

Every now and then while riding, we come upon a little mound of rocks where I have bombarded a rattlesnake to his death. Bill, my husband, calls them "Fay's Monuments," and they are! I don't like to get too close to a snake, and my rock-throwing is amazingly accurate. So I just keep throwing and building my monument until finally the snake is dead. Sometimes though, I have them all covered with rocks before they are dead and have to resort to moving rocks to get them out in the open! This done with a long stick or limb or whatever I can find that is long enough to keep me a good, safe distance from the snake.

We found that rattlesnakes change their locations from time to time. For example, for years they were up in the foothills in the higher part of the valley where we lived, and on the sunny hills where it was rocky. We almost never saw one down on the sagebrush flats. Then suddenly we began seeing them on the flats, mainly along the road in the cool of evening where they would be soaking up the last warmth of the day. Possibly they travel far for water, since it was dry as a bone where we often saw them. Contrary to some thought, they cannot stand a great amount of heat, and they do need water, though they spurn damp or wet areas.

Some people think rattlesnakes won't go through water, but they will. I ran onto one up along a creek southwest of our ranch, and when I got after him he coiled under the creek bank. Then when I left him to get more rocks, he crawled right through the creek, getting all wet and coming out on the other side. I got him anyway, but he did surprise me by going into the water, for I had never seen a rattlesnake do that before.

Some say bullsnakes and rattlesnakes don't live in the same area. I know this to be false, but I have also noticed that we often have a big bullsnake or two around the buildings, but seldom ever see any rattlesnakes near by.

Once up on the home ranch I was fooling with a colt in the corral when a car pulled in. I went over to the pole fence and visited awhile with the party. Suddenly I felt something moving lightly over my boots next to the fence. Actually almost by the time I was aware of its presence it was almost past my boots. It must have had a light tread, but there was one of the biggest bullsnakes I ever saw! I almost shed my boots, but by then the snake was already gone. It wasn't a bit alarmed and perhaps didn't even realize it was "treading on someone else's toes."

When I was a little girl of about 7 or 8, I was riding up in the field east of home when I saw what appeared to be 2 snakes fighting. To this day I wish I had sneaked up slowly to watch, but not thinking, I loped my horse over to see what was going on. It looked to me like a bullsnake and a rattlesnake were fighting, but as soon as I approached they separated and went different directions. I have heard they will fight each other, and possibly this could have settled many an argument, for I have heard as often that they won't. If they were fighting, they were more afraid of the horses than of each other.

Once several years ago when I was at home, my father bought a couple of horses, and they got out one day and headed back for their old home. Someone had seen them going up country along the highway, so we took the truck, expecting to catch them and haul them home. We caught up with them all right, but they had other ideas and we couldn't catch them, not even with oats. So my brother Bert waited up the highway ahead of them while my other brother,

Fred, and I, went back past them, parked the truck and stretched a lariat across the ditch between the truck and the fence. Bert drove them toward the truck while Fred and I waited on the highway close to the truck so they wouldn't run past.

We caught one of the horses in our trap. The other one was one of those smarties that liked to run by and escape, and about the time he saw that his buddy was caught and he was going to be, he turned and started back up the fence. Bert was along the edge of the highway and he sprinted to head and turn the horse. He had the edge on the horse and intended to duck down off the highway into the ditch ahead of him and turn him back. He was really putting on the speed along the side of the road. Now you may not believe it, but that boy suddenly put on the brakes and stopped and turned around right in mid-air and landed back on the road side! And for good reason too, because right about where he would have landed in the ditch was just about the biggest rattlesnake any of us had ever seen. He was all coiled and ready for business too. We don't know if Bert turned the horse back or if the snake did. Anyway he turned back to the truck and we caught him, after killing the snake of course. And I bet Bert saw that snake in his dreams for quite awhile!

Horses' reactions to rattlesnakes differ. Some will spook and shy from them while others will walk right over them. Some horses, if they could see a snake someplace, will shy every time they pass that particular place.

One day I was riding a young mare that I was breaking, up on the high ridge North of my folks' ranch. We were coming down the hill on a rocky trail, and just as the mare stepped onto a big flat rock, I heard a rattlesnake that sounded like it was under that rock. The mare heard it too and she froze right on the spot. It really spooked me, and I kicked her a little too hard. She left that rock like it was hot and almost bucked me off!

A few years ago I was riding up on the hill here at the ranch when I decided to take a look at our yearling colts. I hadn't been close to them in some time, and was wondering how they looked since being turned out. I got the surprise of my life as I neared them! For one thing, I could hear the most horrible casting and choking, and for another thing, the head of the sorrel colt Tuffy, looked almost exactly like a hippo's! I wish we had taken pictures of him because nobody would believe the awful swelling in that colt's nose and mouth. His upper lip hung a full 4 inches below the lower lip, and his lower face was stolen so that it resembled a horse's face not at all.

A buddy of his was in pretty sad shape also, though not nearly as bad as Tuffy. He wasn't so swollen and so wasn't having so much trouble breathing. Tuffy was choking and his nose was running with matter and blood. Then there was a third little face, swollen some, but not seriously.

I didn't know what in the world was wrong. We had been spraying weeds on the range and I thought it might be weed poisoning. I don't know why I didn't think of a rattlesnake. It wasn't until I brought the colts home and Bill said it looked like the work of a snake, that it dawned on me. He had seen horses that were snake-bit before.

Apparently, a cranky old rattlesnake had been disturbed by the sorrel colt, who was bitten in the process and received the largest share of the venom. Then the bay cold came snooping over to see what made his buddy jump, and he got the second bite. The chestnut filly, just as curious, had to take a look and a smell, and she got the third bite. By that time Mr. Snake had probably used up most of his poison.

All 3 colts had fang marks. Tuffy's were very wide apart, partly from the swelling, but it also was evident that the snake had been a big one. The filly had only one fang mark.

We hauled them to the Veterinary Clinic in Ronan, where they were treated much the same as a human being that had been snake-bit. The worst part of it was Tuffy's inability to breathe, and we were afraid he would smother before the swelling left his face. A horse cannot breathe through its mouth for any length of time, as people can. After some shots, we brought the colts home that day, tied them in the barn and carried feed and water to them. Tuffy was hungry because he couldn't grasp anything to eat with that big, fat lip. He didn't appear to be sick at any time however. He could drink, and he did, buckets and buckets of water. With a lot of effort he could worry a little hay into his mouth and then it didn't seem to both him to chew. The filly's swelling began to go down immediately and she was never in any danger, as was the case of the bay colt. Tuffy began to come out of it the next day, and then the swelling fast disappeared. We treated them for several days, and then turned them back on the range when it was certain they were all right.

None of the colts have had any bad after affects of the snake bites. And Tuffy for one, has no fear of rattlesnakes, because one day Bill unknowingly rode him right over one. The snake was in such a hurry to escape the horse's feet that he was too busy to bite.

When I was a girl about 12 or 14, I was feeding the saddle-horses and milk cow one hot summer day. We had big stacks of loose hay then, and they would cut them with a big knife to make it easier to feed one end of the stack without taking the whole top off. This one particular stack was cut from the top down to about half, and we'd been feeding the top part of it. It made sort of a stair step of the end of the stack. Rather than use a ladder I would take off my boots and climb up on the stack barefooted. Then when I was through feeding I would sit on the edge of the stack, turn loose all holds and slide to the ground.

I had been pitching away at this hay, all the time hearing a little buzzing sound much like the sound of a big fly. It bothered me, and I was going to find out what it was. I lifted a flake of hay from the spot above this buzz, and wow! There were two little bitty rattlesnakes, probably just old enough to rattle. Well, I didn't wait around to find out how big or old they were. I threw the pitchfork and this time I didn't slide off the stack; I jumped! From that time on we fed hay of course, but I used the ladder and walked mighty careful, with my boots on. We never did see the snakes again, on the stack, nor around it, though I never did get up on a haystack for a while without thinking about them!

Maybe my closest call with a snake was right here at home. We always thought that this little fellow was lost, that he was brought in with a load of hay. At that time we put up our hay loose, and they had brought a load in on the farmhand to feed the horses at the barn.

We had some wild little kittens at the barn, and I was trying to catch them and make pets of them. I had taken some feed to them on this day, and followed the little yellow one to his hiding place in a corner of the barn. It was here, and there were some old sacks and buckets stacked here that he hid behind. I had a piece of hotcake that I was tempting him with, and stuck my hand in between two buckets where he sat. He watched me, and I coaxed him. Right ahead of him, probably not 6 inches from my hand, was a little rope... I thought. I don't know how long I held my hand there, nor why that little snake didn't bite me. Possibly he was watching the cat. But he rattled just enough for me to realize the "rope" wasn't a rope, but a little rattlesnake. I broke all records falling over backwards and yelled for Bill. He came with a pitchfork and drug the snake out and killed it. It was about 7 or 8 inches long.

It sure used to scare the hay hands when someone would buck in a load of loose hay, raise it up and drop it on the stack... along with a snake of some kind. Chances are it would be a water snake or a grass snake, but it just could be a rattler too!

A friend of ours killed a rattlesnake and thought he would take it with him to play jokes with. He laid the snake on his foot on the tractor, and drove off as big as you please. Something told him to look at the snake, and lucky for him he did, because Mr. Snake was not dead, and was headed right for the tractor boy's bare ankle!

And this same fellow caught a rattlesnake, took him to town for a Saturday night and had himself a lot of fun. He held the snake just behind its head, the body writhing and twisting, as he went from bar to bar. In one bar, an old-time cowboy was drinking. In fact by this time he was pretty drunk. Johnny laid his snake on the bar beside him and settled down to visit. The old cowboy hadn't seen the snake yet, and he laid an arm back along the bar and started to pass time. The snake moved... under his arm. He took one look and they said he almost jerked the doors off leaving the bar.

Johnny caught a mate for his first rattlesnake pet, but he wasn't quite quick enough in nabbing him. It bit him on a finger. He was treated by a doctor and recovered well enough, but it ended his playing with rattlesnakes.

There is much controversy about rattlesnakes. Maybe it will all be settled someday, though I doubt it. Meantime just about everyone agrees that they aren't play things, and we could very well do without them. But then, if they weren't here, perhaps we would have something worse, who knows?

FANNIE STEELE

Bill and I were friends with Frannie. I have attached one of her nice long letters and a couple of her photos.

GRACE LARSON

Helmville, Montana
Feb. 24, 1957

Dear Friends Fay & Bill:

Received your nice long letter of Dec. 15. It sure was nice to hear from you. I would of written before but some how I lost your add. It seems that you told me you were married & that you were going to move to Bitterroot but you didn't give the new add. Well Fay I'm at the same old place doing the same old things, packing hunters back to elk country. I'm fine — still going strong — I can't hardly believe I'll be 70 years young this march 27th don't feel that old. I had to laugh at one of my hunters a couple of years ago. He asked me if I was going to pack the next hunting season & I says, "I guess so if I'm still alive." And he says " "Hell you'll never die." ha! I don't have as many horses as I did, but still have 23 head, but don't raise them any more. I haven't broke any horses for a couple of years, but expect to break one this spring, the only unbroke one I have. He's a gentle little palamino pinto. And last fall a woman from Dillon came to look at him as she wanted a small easy riding saddle horse & also a pinto. My niece was working at a Dude Ranch over there & told her about my pintos. Well any way she bought him, right now at $100.00 and I'm to break him for her for $25.00 & she pays winter pasture till of $15.00 I don't have many summer dudes because I'm alone at ranch & its so hard to get any one that you can depend on to stay here & look after things I could get some fishing parties I know, if I had any help. In hunting season one of my nephews has helped me for a few years. I've had all the hunters I could handle for several years now — any way I've made enough to keep my horses & my self from starving to death.

So you folks are planning on a trip up to the Blackfoot country this summer? Well you just do that & be sure & hunt me up back here in my jungle hideout. My road turns off from Lincoln canyon road about 2 miles from new bridge across Blackfoot river, there's a deserted log house right hand side (toward river) about 100 yrds below where road turns off & you

FAY

come off highway right up a grade + about 3½ miles & you are here. Where a logging road turns off to right, no signs there but keep straight ahead on main traveled road, at next forks of road there's a sign. Well Fay I have never read Bill Huntington's book, which you mentioned in your letter, guess I'll have to buy one of em. Bill K had quite a write up about some in Live stock reporter a few years ago. So you see it's just a short article. A lot of my friends have asked why I don't write a book. I don't think I'm capable of writing one, Fay. A friend of mine is writing on one as a kind of a ghost writer for me. Don't know yet how it's going to turn out. I guess it would sell pretty good because I know so many people around the country and everybody seems to know me. Well its 10 P.M. so I'll finish later.

10:05 Glad to hear you folks are doing O.K. on your good little ranch. I had about 20 head of angus cattle but sold 'em all last fall. I don't raise hay enough here to feed that many + when I put 'em out on feed in winter it's $10.00 a head per month here in valley + at the low prices it just wouldn't pay to keep them. I winter my horses over in Helena valley at $3.00 a head per month but he don't feed them. So Bill is a horse trader, eh? Well I used to like to trade horses too. It's fun when you don't get beat too bad. Good saddle horses are selling good so I hear. I'm like you folks about farm machinery, tractors + etc. The good old horses are best. It's hard these days to find a hired man who knows how to harness a team, let alone drive one. Last summer I mowed all the hay with a team + had a neighbor rake + bale it + then I used jeep to haul it out of field, thot it would be quicker, as I was alone. Yes, I think a person is always busy on a ranch + as you say the days aren't long enough, to do the things you want to do. Glad your mom + dad are doing well. Maybe I did give them a little dog, I know we give away a lot of them. When you see, or write to them tell them hello for me. They should come over this way too + take a look at our new highway + also stop in + say hello, sure changes the looks of the country and a very pretty road. Where is your folks ranch, near Hotsprings. Very nice + a girl from Missouri + myself were over to Plains last spring to see my older brother who is a blacksmith there. If I get over that way again I'll try + swing around *your way & say hello.③ I like horse folks & also angus cattle and would like to your ranch & live stock. Yes, I heard all about Jake a couple of years ago. And this last fall he wrote to me from Ft. Harrison, after he read article in Farmer, and when I took my horses over to pasture first of Dec. my niece & her boy took me out to see him, he was so happy to see me, we could hardly get away. He had some rodeo pictures he wanted us to see.④ I sure feel sorry for him, he said he liked to see people who talked his language. There was only old men in his ward & he was so darn lonesome for someone to talk to. He sent a Xmas card & I sent him one. But haven't heard from him since. He thot that the Dr. at the Ft. was helping him, but from what I hear it's pretty bad & no cure. The Dr. himself has it, but he can't get around fairly good Jake told us. He seemed to be cheerful, we was joking bout the good looking nurses and he says "I never had much luck with the women" "and I never got married because none of 'em ever ask me." Well this letter is getting to be a book itself so I'll say so long for now, surely did enjoy your letter so send me another. Yes, I am alone & yes I'm always alone in the winter time. And last summer I was alone up un-till hunting season — but I do have lots of company in the summer. I can't afford to hire any one to stay, nor can I talk any one into staying just for their board, so that's that. My best wishes to you both_____ and I'll be looking for you this summer._____ Fannie*

Fannie Sperry Steele, was born Fannie Sperry March 27, 1887. She died February 11, 1983. Fannie was a bronc rider from Montana. She was one of the first women inducted into the National Rodeo Hall of Fame in Oklahoma in 1975. She became the first Montana native in the National Cowgirl Hall of Fame in 1978.

Fannie was born in the Beartooth Mountains of Montana to Rachel and Datus Sperry. She was a first-generation Montanan. Her mother, Rachel, taught her to ride before she could walk. Fannie's father wasn't able to ride due to an old injury. She was the only woman to ride her entire career without tying her stirrups under the horse's belly. This was a practice rodeo judges allowed women. Fannie inherited her love of horses, especially Pintos, from her mother. She won several awards for her riding in professional rodeos; the Women's Bucking Horse Champion of Montana in 1904 when she was 17, and Lady Bucking Horse Champion of the World at the first Calgary Stampede rodeo in 1912. Fannie had ridden the horse Red Wing, a wild bronc who had trampled fellow rider Joe LaMar to death only days earlier. Fannie won $1,000 cash and a silver-mounted saddle worth $250, and a belt buckle plated with gold valued at $300.

Fannie rode the famous bronc, Midnight. She was one of a few that rode him. Midnight was known as a horse that had never been ridden. She won the bronc riding event in Pendleton, Oregon, Miles City, Montana, Helmville, Montana, the Winnipeg Stampede in Canada, and so many other rodeos throughout the West.

She was inducted into the National Cowboy Hall Of Fame in 1975.

Fannie married Bill Steele, a fellow rodeo rider, producer, and arena clown, on April 30, 1913. They operating their own Wild West show and also performed with the Miller Brothers' and Irwin Brothers' Wild West Shows. Besides her horsemanship, Fannie was also skilled with a rifle. Her husband trusted her to shoot a cigar out of his mouth!

Sperry Steele competed for the last time in 1925 at Bozeman, Montana, and continued riding exhibitions into her 50s. Fannie and Bill became stock contractors, near Helena, providing horses and bulls for rodeos all over the West. She also became one of four women in the US who were licensed outfitter-guides. She did not completely retire from her outfitter-guide trips into the mountains until 1974when she was 87. Her last years were spent in a rest home in Helena, Montana. She died on February 11,1983 at the age of 96. Her husband, Bill, died in 1935.

JUNE COX

The Intermountain Quarter Horse September 1977

June Cox is no longer a rodeo headliner. She has turned her unusual talents to every day affairs such as operating her own ranch in Lincoln County, Nevada, and raising three sons. Now, instead of following the rodeo circuit, June is a cattle raiser, a farrier, a fence builder, a butcher, a baker, and an alfalfa hay raiser.

Not too many years ago her name was synonymous with the excitement of the rodeo arena. Sometimes June officiated, but most of the time she participated. As her reputation grew, fans felt no rodeo should start without her. June took the World Title goat tying at the Girls International Rodeo League (G.I.R.L.) World Championship in Calgary, Alberta, Canada, in 1967. The following year she won the G.I.R.L. Title in both calf roping and goat tying winning two more saddles. This event was also at Calgary. The next year at the G.I.R.L Championship Finals at Red Deer, Alberta, Canada, she ended the year winning the calf roping title again. Finally she became president of G.I.R.L.

All of this was before her accident. At the age of 34, June's rodeo career was finished.

It happened at a horse show in Ely, Nevada, August 9, 1970. June's quarter horse stallion, Poco Piute, was nearing the finish of a quarter mile stock horse race. The powerful stallion was in a "dead run."

Suddenly, a stroke caused the horse to lose control of his front legs. Before an astonished audience, Poco Piute flipped over completely pinning June under 1100 pounds of frightened animal. The saddle horn and cantle crushed into June's shoulder and head.

The crazed horse tried to regain his footing. He tried and fell three times and three times Poco Piute fell back on his unconscious rider's back and legs.

June's friends rushed to her aid and managed to get the stricken horse away from her.

June had 14 breaks in her right arm, shoulder and chest. June's face was covered in blood, her right eye hung from its socket.

The seriousness of June's injuries were so severe that she was flown to St. Marks Hospital, in Salt Lake City, Utah, where she would obtain the extensive care she would require if she lived.

A lump of bandages on the bedsheet, June slowly regained consciousness. Whispering through broken jaws, she asked first about her horse. She later learned that Poco Piute was no longer able to be ridden.

This was a sad ending for such fine animal. On him, June had won boxes of ribbons, nearly two dozen trophies, silver engraved spurs, five saddles and 14 buckles. He was priceless to her.

Poco Piute died the following spring and was buried on June's eighty-acre ranch, seven miles north of Caliente, Nevada.

After two days in the hospital June began to show improvement. Doctors felt she would not only live, but surgery on her injured face could now begin.

June's face was so swollen one could not tell what she should look like. The plastic surgeon asked for a photograph of June to see how she had looked before the accident. Since one was not obtainable he performed the delicate 4.5-hour operation without a picture to guide him.

Still the surgery proved successful in reconstructing her face. Only tiny hairline scars around her soft hazel eyes and one on her chin show any signs of her ordeal.

Most important, June's vision remained as good as before. Her right arm, which doctors feared would be permanently damaged, was well once again. Along with therapy June's self-determination proved invaluable.

Carolyn June Wilkin was born on June 16, 1936, in the small mining town of Pioche, Nevada. She was one of seven children raised by her parents Robert and Della Wilkin.

June was born with a love of horses. She often helped her neighbor "Slim" with his horses. The busy cowboy appreciated June's natural ability with the horses. He taught his young friend how to ride.

Before long June showed herself to be a good hand at helping him break the "green" horses into good mounts.

June reflects on those years; "Being around horses meant lots of happy hours for me. But in my heart I longed for a horse of my own. It was hard for me to work with a new horse just until it was gentle and then give it up."

At fourteen the young teenage girls' dream came true. Friends of her family presented June with her own horse. It was a young mustang filly June named Penny. June's experience came in handy with her own mare. This time she would not have to say "goodbye" to a horse that she loved.

Along with her love of horses, June also had regular schoolgirl activities. She also had a few rather unconventional activities.

In her senior year at Lincoln County High School, June became the first female school bus driver. Early objections from some parents soon disappeared as this young lady proved to be a good driver. Even the unusually noisy din of a crowded bus was kept to a fairly low pitch, demonstrating the respect her fellow students had for her.

June states, "I felt the value of work at an early age. During grade school I was a Grit Paper sales girl. Through high school I worked as a clerk and cashier at the Gem Theater. I was also a telephone operator on the weekends and at night and still managed to sandwich in a column for the Pioche Record newspaper."

"I worked during school and during summer months, too, selling greeting cards."

June remembers along with being a bus driver she also had three other part-time jobs at the same time.

In high school June studied typing shorthand and bookkeeping along with her required subjects. When she graduated, she was hired as a private secretary for the Morris Motor Company in Pioche.

On May 30, 1955, June moved to Ely, Nevada, taking her mare with her. She was employed as secretary for the Kennecott Copper Corporation in nearby McGill, Nevada. Again displaying her versatility she worked for the same company as a PBX operator.

During the next seven years June finally realized her dream to live on a ranch.

June also joined the Ely Riding Club and the McGill Riding and Roping Club. In March of 1956 she trained her mare to work a rope.

"At long Last," she said, "I roped a calf from my own horse and went down the rope and tied the calf, just as it is down in professional rodeos. Was I thrilled! After two months practice I got the chance to rope exhibition at the Helldorado Rodeo. Riding a borrowed horse, I roped and tied my calf in:17.02 seconds before backed grandstands. My time matched that of a cowboy who won fourth place money that day."

What a start to June's rodeo dreams. During the following years, June roped and barrel raced at all the rodeo's she could. Behind the rodeo scenes many surprised cowboys gazed at June while the pretty cowgirl shod her own horse. At that time women farriers were certainly the exception. But she learned horse shoeing to get her horse shod properly and at the right time.

Those were thrilling days for June. She recalls, "It was exciting in rodeo. Winning events makes one really proud because the competition is so keen. The teamwork between horse and rider is important."

In 1959, June married William Alvin Cox, also a rodeo contestant. Alvin worked for Kennecott along with June. Together the couple competed in rodeos on weekends and during vacations.

On a trip to Idaho for a rodeo where both June and her husband were competing June first learned of all the girls rodeos. She said, "I could hardly wait to get to Homedale, Idaho, next weekend where the all girl rodeo would be. It was great to be able to compete against women for a change."

This was the beginning of another adventure. June arranged her work schedule so she could enter rodeos during their trips. June's winning on the circuit paid for her family trips, as well as helping to pay for extras for the family.

Sadly, after 10 years of marriage, June was divorced. Soon after, in 1970, she suffered her fateful accident.

June how lives with her sons Daniel Alvin, 17; Clinton Jay, 15; and Bert Lynn, 12, on their 75 acre ranch.

June is a good cook. She prepares delicious meals for her family from their own home raised products such as meat, milk, and eggs.

June also enjoys showing city children who visit the ranch where milk really comes from. The children are fascinated to watch how milk gets from cow to pail by hand.

June does everything pertaining to her ranch herself including bothering her own beef. She does this to keep prices down. She also sells cattle, sheep, goats, and hay.

Some feel that this lifestyle is not quite right for a woman. It is bone-tiring work that demands long hours from sunrise to long after dark. June Cox could sleep past sunrise and go to work in an air-conditioned office. She has the skill. But she chose ranch life. Here she can realize a long-time dream come true. June has recently acquired 40 acres of undeveloped brush land that she and her sons are working on to get ready to plant and build an arena. This will be a place where June can share her riding and roping skills with young people. "Sharing knowledge with others never takes away frm oneself. It helps me to grow as a person," June states. June's many experiences in life have helped her to realize that life must have goals in order to be fulfilling. Since her near brush with death, she believes that God saved her life for a mission yet to be accomplished. She states, "Working with young people could be it."

June Cox is a faithful member of the Church of Jesus Christ of Latter-day Saints. She is gifted with a lovely alto singing voice that blends beautifully with the Church choir. She also plays the piano.

Besides singing, June is professionally capable of doing fine hand tooling in leather. An exquisite leather clock, carved by June, is proudly displayed on her living room wall. Recently June and her sons built an addition to their home, doubling its size and adding a fireplace.

Following the death of her stallion, Poco Piute, June bred her mares to Chip Wilkin, by Chip O'Buzz, by Buzzy H. He is owned by June's brother, Gary Wilkin, of St. George, Utah. June is now getting many fine foals from these crosses. She also states that these colts have the best dispositions and are the easiest to break and train of any horses that she has ever worked with and not one of them has ever offered to kick.

June bred her mare, Gibbs Bar Blair, by Bar Blair, and Leo Bar to Chip Wilkin. This breeding produced Chip Bar Wilkin, a palomino colt, in 1974. June is now breeding some mares to him and has already received three foals this year. June is excited with a buckskin filly by Chip Wilkin that arrived this year. The filly is out of Jule's Julie Bar, a half-sister to Gibbs Bar Blair.

Along with her own horses, June boards many for others. She is now in the process of training three appaloosa yearlings for Richard Tam of Las Vegas, Nevada. These colts are for sale and are from top quality appaloosa mares bred to a thoroughbred stallion.

June takes advantage of opportunities that come her way. She recently boarded, with the intention of breeding, Big Red Sonoita, a son of Dick Sonoita, a superior AQHA Halter and Steer Roping Horse with an ROM in Reining. Big Red is owned by Jim Lee of Las Vegas, Nevada, who purchased him in Oklahoma.

June's son Clint gives a clear picture of his mother when he states, "Mom still manages to raise hay, raise cows, raise sons, and try not to raise prices."

Cowgirl June Cox

JUNE COX, CHAMPION ALL-AROUND COWGIRL

Born in Pioche, Nevada in 1936, June Wilkin was one of a family of seven children. Only June and her brother Gray, were rodeo-minded, but their father, Robert Wilkin used to rodeo in his younger days. Familiar with mining, he began to work in the mines around Pioche, and today he and a son, Joe, just older than June, are partners in the Wilkin Mining and Trucking Company.

June was fond of horses from the beginning, but had no chance to ride very much until she was about ten years old. She borrowed a gentle mare belonging to a neighbor who broke horses, and later she rode some of the gentler colts he was breaking. She was a natural with horses, and nothing pleased her more than to teach a green colt something useful.

Then came the spring of 1949, and June got a horse of her very own! A bunch of horses had been gathered off the range for shipment, and there was a little filly that was too young to ship. So it was given to June, just a little bay mustang filly with a star on her forehead, but a treasure to a little girl who loved horses.

One of June's daily chores was to lead Penney, as the filly was called, to water. She soon tired of leading her new charge, and hopped on one day, only to take a bucking horse ride she wouldn't soon forget. Before she bucked off, the filly stopped, and June, proud as punch, decided that was a lot of fun. She was soon riding Penney daily, and eventually trained her for barrel racing, trail classes, calf roping, team roping, and Western pleasure.

In the summer of 1950, June was grounded for some time with a ruptured appendix. What she missed most during this time was her horse, and the chance to ride.

June was interested in sports in school, and played on the girls' softball and basketball teams. Since her father was in the trucking business, she learned to drive truck, and when bids were let for a bus driver from Pioche to Panaca, she applied for the job and got it. Her pay was $100 a month, which was very good, since she had to go to school anyway, and preferred driving to just riding along. At the time she was a senior in high school.

Always ambitious, June worked through school whenever she could, and held jobs as cashier and candy and popcorn girl in the local theater, and later she was a switchboard operator in the telephone office. During the summer she added to her chores, copywriter, reporter and secretary for the Pioche Record, holding all these jobs until the telephone office asked her to work full-time. During school, she worked on weekends and after school hours.

After graduating she went to work for Morris Motor Company as a secretary, and the next summer got a job at the Kennecott Corporation as secretary to the construction superintendent.

By this time June lived on a ranch for the first time. The owner, Mary Fields, also worked at Kennecott, and the two commuted back and forth together. June had Penney and one of her colts with her.

And she was attending horse shows, rodeos, and the Saddle Club events, and had been the Queen of Pioche Lion's Club Rodeo one year. It was at a rodeo in McGill, Nevada that she met her future husband, Alvin Cox, who was competing in bareback riding, saddle bronc riding, and bull riding. She and Alvin team-roped together, and she barrel raced and roped on his horse Smokey. It was while riding Smokey that she won her first trophy in the barrel race at Ely, Nevada, in 1956.

Alvin was working at Kennecott then, but was drafted in 1957. In 1959, he and June were married at the LDS Temple in St. George, Utah, and they drove to Ft. Eustis, Virginia on their honeymoon. He was stationed there at the time. Shortly afterwards, Alvin received his discharge, and the couple drove home by way of Oklahoma, where they picked up a new two-horse trailer.

Upon returning to McGill, they both went back to work at Kennecott, and at the same time operated the LDS Church farm. They spent most of their race time riding and roping with the McGill Roping Club.

In the spring of 1962, they got a new trailer home, their pride and joy. In June of 1964, they were heartbroken when fire destroyed their home, most of their personal belongings, and all their prized trophies and ribbons, except one, a trophy won by Alvin and his father earlier when they raised and showed purebred sheep.

Leather work is a hobby as well as a business with Alvin and June, and the saddle she rides was made by Alvin.

The lure of the rodeo was drawing June like a magnet during their early years of marriage. Nobody tried harder or had more courage and heart than June, and the competition, excitement and challenge became a part of her life. From the time she learned to rope from her brother Gray, practicing on bales of hay, buckets, the milkcow calf, or whatever was handy, calf roping was her big thrill. She worked hard, studied and listened, and finally felt capable of traveling and competing. She roped her first calf before a large audience at the Helldorado Rodeo at Las Vegas, with a time of 17.2 on a horse she borrowed from Sam Fancher. From then on her record at rodeos and shows would almost fill a book.

They needed a better horse for June, and purchased a registered Quarter Horse stallion, Poco Piute from Neil Larson, McGill, Nevada. A 3 year old, Poco was broke to ride, and June and Alvin continued his training. He became a horse that willingly works any event they ask of him, and he also is a gentle mount for the three little Cox boys; Danny, born in 1960, Clint in 1962, and Bert in 1965.

When June began rodeoing, miles meant nothing to her and money was secondary, Her travels range from ten to fifteen thousand miles a year.

She has won 14 trophies in all; in barrel racing, ladies trail classes, Western pleasure, pole bending, calf roping, and team roping. She and Poco also received a trophy for winning the quarter of a mile saddle horse race in Ely inn 1963, and one for traveling the farthest to the Canadian All-Girl Rodeo at Calgary in 1966. She has contested in 6 states and in Canada.

In 1961, Ely, Nevada held its first all-girl rodeo, and June was on hand, entered in all 6 events, bareback riding, cow riding, calf roping, ribbon roping, steer undecorating and barrel racing. She placed in 5 or the 6, and won her first all-around championship buckle.

She ended that year by winning the Idaho Girls' Rodeo Association bareback championship, second in calf roping, fifth in ribbon roping, seventh in undecorating, and third in the all around.

In 1963, June widened her scope of travel to include Montana, where she competed in Montana's first all-girl rodeo at Hot Springs. Here she won the all-around championship, and upon returning to the Treasure State later that summer, she won the all-around championship at Ronan's all-girl rodeo. She had been skeptical about contesting and traveling clear to Montana, but after visiting and competing there, she felt very much at home and said "I think I would like to live in Montana."

June began the 1964 rodeo season with a flash by winning the all-around championship at the all-girl rodeo in Murphy, Idaho, and from there she went north to Brewster, Washington where she was runner-up to the champion.

At Ellensburg, Washington on May 24 that year, she was second in ribbon roping and 4th in goat tying, and she bucked off her cow. Luck wasn't with June at Ellensburg, but she made up for it at the next weekend when she journeyed to her lucky state of Montana. She was the all-around champion at the Missoula all-girl rodeo, winning a beautiful $150 silver and gold buckle.

Her next trip was to Walla Walla, Washington, where she took all her stock the first day, planning on a jump to Hot Springs, Montana the next day. She had her work set out for her that weekend, and she approached it with her usual zest, winning second in the average in ribbon roping, a third day money in cow riding (she bucked off her second cow,) and she won the first go-round in goat tying, but her second goat got up, a big disappointment to June.

On to Hot Springs, and after an all-night drive, June and Poco were right in the middle of rodeo competition again, winning the calf roping, fourth in the goat tying, and first in bareback riding, plus the all-around championship honors.

And the next weekend found her in Smelterville, Idaho, tying for first in cow riding and third in goat tying.

About a month later June was riding a mare at home when it reared over backwards with her, seriously injuring her back, and she was laid up for the rest of the season. Another injury June tells about occurred when she was first "tromped" by a bareback bronc at a rodeo in Glenns Ferry, Idaho. She came out of this with a lot of bruises and a broken rib.

At Walla Walla in 1965, a cow fell with her and injured her quite seriously, which June claims, ended her rodeo riding career. She says, "I will compete in the timed events from now on, and leave the rough stuff to the younger girls."

In spite of a new baby that spring, and her injuries, June ended the 1965 season with the ribbon roping championship of the Girls Northwest Rodeo Association, 9th in barrel racing, 4th in goat tying, and 8th in the all-around standings. She said it had been quite a struggle.

1967 may go down as the happiest and most successful yet, and possibly the busiest. 2 trips to Calgary, a trip to Lethbridge, and several runs into Idaho and Washington, and June emerged the winner of a beautiful trophy saddle at the G.I.R.L. Finals at the Stampede Corral in Calgary, in September this year. This saddle was awarded to her for the championship in goat tying for the season. The G.I.R.L. is a newly-formed girls' rodeo association for Canadian and US contestants, and most of the girl rodeos in both countries were G.I.R.L.-approved, so June's points at these rodeos went toward the final standings. Early in the year she had joined the Girls International Rodeo League with an eye on at least one championship saddle.

With all her traveling, June still finds time to work at home on improving their ranch and ground. They have planted several acres in grain, with plans for permanent pasture late, for hay and grazing. Since Alvin works steady for the Wilkin Mining and Trucking firm, much of the work at home falls on June, and she can work the fields with a TD 6 Caterpillar or build a corral, in between caring for the children and rodeoing. Soon she and Alvin plan on building a new arena, and will train horses (they have some registered Quarter Horse mares,) raise a few goats and calves, sheep and milk cows.

A busy cowgirl, an all-around top hand, June Cox will be long remembered after she leaves the rodeo arena!

CIRCLIN' CLOSE

Published in October 1973 Quarter Horse Digest

The season's Championship is fast approaching, and it looks as though Patty Ann Carraher of Anaconda, is having a runaway in Montana Barrel Race standings. Patty won the State a couple of years ago and late as it is, it is doubtful if anyone can catch her for the 1973 Championship. She is riding a sorrel gelding Rivets Bar, son of our Jule Bar, and out of the sorrel mare Quarter Ann, and this was the same horse that she won most of her 1971 points on.

In runner-up spots so far is Rinda Ogilvie, Florence, one of the younger members of MBRA. Rinda usually rides the Palomino horse Palabar, by Leo Bar, one of the most honest and faithful horses on the circuit, and a horse that has only one eye. Rinda has been real tough competition all season, and she has a lead of about two hundred dollars over her mother, Ethel, at this time. Joey Waples is in fourth position with a sizable lead over fifth place girl, Kay Fowlie. Kay, a college rodeo contestant, is one of the top barrel racers in the country also.

Darlene Collins won the Great Falls Barrel race this year. Darlene is the former Darlene Swanson of Augusta, and several years ago she was one of the "toughs" in barrel racing when she was mounted on her beautiful sorrel mare, Miss Cranky Skip. Zale Olson of Fairfield was second at Great Falls; Patty Ann was third, and fourth was split between Ethel Ogilvie and Linda Peth, of Bow, Washington.

Faye Olsen won Libby this year, and Sidney won by Ethel Ogilvie. Patty Ann won Glasgow; young sister Terri Kaye Carraher won Townsend, and GRA member, Lila Mae Stewart of Missoula, won Helena. Lila Mae also won all 3 go-rounds and the average at Kalispell.

Phyllis Brosz is leading the MRA standings to date, with Kay Fowlie in second position. Kay won East Helena, and has a fine action picture on the cover of the July issue of MRA's Chute Boss publication.

Lila Glade has a new baby girl, and Bobbie Meiwald is expecting. More barrel racers for future rodeos!

Jan Wagner was visiting her parents at the Kalispell Fair and Rodeo, and her mother, Irene Walter, was happy to see her leave her home in eastern Montana. Why? Because Jan was expecting a call from the stork at any time. Husband Terry was rodeoing at Kalispell, but Jan only got to watch the barrel race event, the first time she has missed running at her hometown rodeo in a long time.

We were real sorry to learn of the death of Ronnie Anderson's good young brown filly. Ronnie had only started her on barrels, and she had high hopes for next year. The filly was out of Ronnie's old brown mare, Cotton Jet by Cotton M.

Jumpy Jule has won his Superior barrel points in AQHA shows, one of the first horses in the Northwest to do so.

Jumpy thinks he died and went to Heaven lately, since we have been so busy house-building and trying to move that he seldom gets caught. The old fellow (he is eleven) never looked better than he does this year. Jumpy was by our Jule Bar.

Judy Myllymaki of Arlee, won the Missoula Fair barrel race this year, on her bay mare, Palleo Polly by Palleo Pete. This mare is getting to be a real threat to the barrel racers, and she is a top of heeling horse for Judy in the Team Roping event.

Lila Mae Stewart won second at the Fair, and third and fourth was a tie between Iva Ivey, Kalispell, and Terri Kaye Carraher, Anaconda. Iva is working their racehorse on barrels now, and when he gets some experience, he is going to be double-tough. Sired by Bar Blair (by Leo Bar,) and out of a daughter of Bob's Folly, this horse did well at the track, and if Iva works him like she has her brown horse Bushkey, everyone will have to whip up. Iva is the grandmother of 5.

Sharon Matt of Arlee, has added barrel racing to her rodeo events (she is a good team roper, either head or heel,) and she made a nice run at the Fair to win third in the children's barrel race. Sharon is fourteen, and teamed with her brother Shorty, has made some real shiny runs in the team-roping event.

SCOTT LYNCH

The best thing in the horse line that ever happened to Scott Lynch of Ronan, was the purchase of Jule Bar Reed, 4-year old gelding by Jule Bar (Sugar Bars-Juleo,) and out of Wilson's Reed Lady 11 (Red Nugget-Wilson's Reed Lady) This little bald faced bay gelding was not too well broke to ride when Scott started roping calves on him. He ended the 1972 season tied for runner-up spot in the MQHA, and Scott roped many a calf on "Baldy" or "Baby Horse" as he is more commonly called, in rodeos, and jackpots, last year.

With some 39 ropings behind them, this pair missed only 3 calves in competition during the season, quite a record for a 4-year-old colt; so with a year's experience behind him, 1973 looks mighty bright for this outstanding youngster and his owner-rider. Scott is a new member of the MQHA, and lives near Ronan with his wife and 3 children.

Scott didn't start out with the high caliber horses that the youth of this day rides. His father bought him an old Albino stallion in a sale ring when Scott was going to high school. The old horse was nearly blind, and when the sun was high he could barely see where to put his next foot, but somehow he began to rely on Scott for guidance, and the pair of them won all-around cowboy honors two different years at St. Ignatius. Scott was badly bitten by the roping bug by that time, and with a lot of hard work and perseverance, he got to the point where he could rope a little in competition. But he was always just short of the top because he was never mounted on a horse that had quick, early speed to get him to his calf in a hurry. That is, not until he bought the little bald-faced horse that has become his favorite roping pardner. "Baldy" looked pretty small during his first year on the road, but no one fully realized just how small he was until Scott put him on the scales in February, this spring, when he was coming 5 years old. Scott and his outfit weigh around 240 pounds or thereabouts, and Baldy, grown up quite a lot by 1973, tipped the scales, saddle and all, at a hefty 1050 pounds! So his 4-year-old size was not much over 3 times that of his rider and outfit. That little horse was packing quite a load, without having to come to a dead stop with a calf bouncing on the end of his rope. Sometimes he was up against calves that were over a third of his weight, but Baldy never seemed to have much of a problem taking care of his end of the business.

 And he remained cool under stress. At the Hamilton Bitterroot Indoor arena, Scott roped his calf, and it got into a corner with Baldy right up on it, and a lot of slack in the rope. This is trouble for any roper, and it could have been serious this night. So far Baldy had no bad habits, and he didn't know what it was like to run off with a calf dragging behind him. He was in a storm this night, but despite his fright and indecision, he kept his eyes on Scott from the time the cowboy left the saddle until he got hold of the calf. Baldy had a front leg over the rope and this panicked him further, yet the little fellow backed as well as he could on the rope, eyes on Scott every instant, until the calf was tied. Many a seasoned rope horse would have tried to run off.

 At the Winter Fair in Bozeman this year, Scott missed his first loop, and just as the calf bounced off the back of the arena, he roped it with the 2nd loop. The calf ran behind some poles in the corner, and there was Baldy, jumping from side to side like a cutting horse as the calf would duck one way and then the other. Finally the calf got out of the cover so that Scott could throw and tie him, and Baldy was backing on the rope like a veteran, doing his job as always.

WRONG BUNDLE

The Homestead Capitol Days in our area were very much the same as they were in any part of the country. Times were hard then and people had little in the way of luxuries and entertainment. They worked hard for what they had, and they were mostly honest, decent people who didn't ask for nor expect much more than a living for themselves and their families.

They were far from town usually, but had a schoolhouse in their midst, and most of the children attending these schools came either on horseback or on foot; sometimes they drove a team or a single horse to a wagon or a buggy.

People made their own entertainment, and dances were held quite often in the schoolhouse or in someone's home, and the entire neighborhood would show up to enjoy the fun and music, which often lasted clear through the night. And many times not only the immediate neighbors would be there, but people from as far as 20 or 30 miles away would come. No one at that time thought anything about the distance. They would dance and visit and play all night, and head for home the next day.

Visiting was generally done by horseback or wagon also, and one of our neighbors tells an amazing story about this.

One hot, sunny summer day she and her husband and tiny baby were going visiting some of the neighbors. They had horses saddled and ready, and Mother had a bag with extra diapers, bottle, and other necessities for the baby. She mounted her horse, and her husband handed the baby to her, and as an after thought, returned to the house to get an umbrella. The sun was beating down so hard, and they wanted to shelter the baby.

Her horse was gentle, but didn't know anything about umbrellas, and when that thing shot open, he started to jump. Of course she had both hands full and could have used another hand. The horse started to buck down the hill that ran from the house to the barns and pens, and Mother, fearing for her baby, decided she would have to unload something in a hurry. So she dropped one of her bundles and jerked the horse to a stop.

Finally quieting the horse, she heard her baby cry away back up the hill, and not until then did she realize she had dropped the baby instead of the diaper bag! Luckily the little tot was unhurt, but its mother took a lot of kidding around the neighborhood.

FIZZ ALL AROUND CONTENDER

The Quarter Horse Journal: Fizz February 1966

Often seen in shows and rodeos but not so often mentioned are the good Quarter Horse geldings of this horse world. Among these "specials" is the brown horse Fizz, owned by Leo and Anita Woodbury, Geyser, Montana.

Fizz was foaled July 2, 1958, at Arbon, Idaho, on the ranch of the well-known horseman, D. T. (Sod) Williams. His sire was Sizzler by Oklahoma Star, and his dam was Poco Dixiecrat by Poco Rojo. A real handsome, well-built horse, Fizz has the action of a cat and has been going great guns in the arena for some time. It was back in the spring of 1960 that Leo and Anita took a mare of theirs to the Williams' station Poco Star, and while there they inquired about a calf roping prospect. Sod showed them Fizz, then a real lanky two-year-old, and Leo had this to say about the brown cold: "Right away I took a liking to him. He looked, in my opinion, like a calf horse should."

Fizz's dam is a half-sister to Poco Star, which also attracted the attention of the Woodburys, and they brought him home in early May of 1960 and turned him into pasture for the rest of the summer.

That fall, Leo got the colt up and started to ride him. For some time he acted just like any average colt of good breeding, learning well and showing intelligence. Then, as his training progressed, he impressed Leo by always being in the right place at the right time, with his feet under him like an old horse.

Leo didn't crowd his new colt, but worked him easy and slow, starting him with a hackamore and riding him that way or with a snaffle until the spring when he was five. The Woodbury Ranch consists of some 25,000 acres, and there are a lot of cattle on a spread of that size so Fizz had all the cow work anyone could want for a young horse. He followed many a cow for many a mile and headed or heeled a lot of critters for doctoring or other reasons before he was ever taken into an arena.

The spring he was four, a veterinarian gave him an intravenous shot and missed the jugular vein. The drug caused the tissue between the skin and muscles of the horses' neck to slough, and this drained for over two months. He was given so many shots of combiotic and other drugs prescribed by different people, that when Leo went back to catch him, Fizz would break out in a small sweat and run around and around the corral, trying to escape what he termed torture. To this day he gets pretty nervous and excited, and it is believed these shots had a lot to do with it. Only when an old-time horseman, Walt Perry of Missoula, prescribed a remedy did Fizz respond and recover in short time.

When Fizz was five, Leo starting hauling him to rodeos with his regular rope horse. In July 1963 he took both horses to the state Quarter Horse show in Deer Lodge, entering Fizz in the roping and reining. This was Fizz's first show of any kind, but he won the first go-round in reining and tied for third and fourth in roping. This was all the encouragement Leo needed, and he started contesting on Fizz from then on.

Their next rodeo and show was Filer, Idaho, where they rode at night and have the horse show events in the afternoon. Fizz again brought home the honors by winning the working cowhorse class and the reserve Champion Working horse title of the show. In the open horse show he won the reining and barrel racing.

Woodburys don't go to very many horse shows, being busy ranching and rodeoing, but Fizz has won or placed almost every time he has contested at shows. In 1964 at the Great Falls Quarter Horse show, he won the roping and reining and was Reserve Champion Working Horses. He also received his Register of Merit in arena performance in 1964 and won the Rope Horse of the Year trophy for the state of Montana. He was placing well in the roping at rodeos during this time as well.

By this time, Anita was contesting on him by the barrel racing event regularly. She had her troubles, the same as with any new barrel horse, but they were comparatively few. Since Fizz was a bright pupil, he caught on fast. In the summer of 1965 Anita was giving the girls a run for their money for the Montana State Championship in barrel racing, when Fizz seriously injured his left hind fetlock joint. This put him out of the running altogether as far as any work was concerned, and he was laid off the rest of the year.

Fizz has always hauled and traveled well. He is at home wherever he stops, and the way of rodeo seems to agree with him, as it does with his "family," the Woodburys.

Leo's rodeo experience began when he contested in high school rodeos. Practically raised on a horse, it was only natural that he chose a life among horses and cattle. He and Anita attended school together and were married in 1956. It was with Leo's encouragement that she started seriously thinking about barrel racing, and Anita has become one of the top contestants in the country.

So when Fizz is unloaded at a rodeo, he knows his day won't be over until calf roping and barrel racing events are over. And he'll work each event with ease, giving his best. Very often a horse will perform well at one event but become confused if asked to work another, especially when these events are practically simultaneous. But Fizz is wise, and whether it's a calf he is looking for or a barrel, you can be sure he sees it and knows what to do.

Leo and Anita have three children, Leo, Cindy, and Russ. All of these youngsters ride and have ridden since they were babies. It is very common to see the two oldest ones exercising horses in the arenas or around racetracks, riding their little saddles with the confidence of a born rider. They will get plenty of practice on the ranch, with all those cattle and some fifteen Quarter Horse broodmares with colts to take care of. Woodbury's stallion is the chestnut son of Leo Bar, Beau Bar, a horse that will work a rope, run the barrels, or babysit the kids.

Fizz is coming along fine on that bad leg now, and Woodburys plan to have him ready to go to work again when the next season's rodeos and shows begin. They'll miss him plenty if he isn't, but it is hoped that this good and faithful brown gelding will be back on the job in 1966. If he is, look out you calf ropers, barrel racers, and reinsmen for ol' Fizz sure has a lot of lost time to make up for. And he is just the horse that can do it!

STORMY BOY

May 1968

Stormy Boy, the Pride of the Nauman Ranch! There is nothing a saddle-horse can do that he can't do, and a little better job than most. Stormy believes that honesty is the best policy, and he has been making an honest effort to please for many years. He just seldom does anything wrong; that is, once he is caught. For Stormy is about the world's worst when it comes to being caught. He just doesn't like it. Maybe it is a game, to see just how long he can evade his pursuers. Because once he is haltered, he is the gentlest, most obedient horse the Nauman's have on the place. And they can (usually) forgive him for this aggravating habit once he is under saddle and working. But one time especially Bill and Nona were anything but happy with Stormy. Bill had gone to catch him in the corral, and as he started to bridle him, the horse jerked away and ran through four gates. After Bill spent more than an hour trying to get up to the horse, he finally had to give up in disgust, and went to the house to get his wife's help. Nona wasn't angry (yet) and possibly she could get the job done. It took her quite a while, but finally she did get up to stormy and bridled him.

The horse was foaled on August 15, 1950 at the Vic Anderson Ranch near Cascade, Montana. Once dark gray, he is now nearly white, and his record is the envy of many good horsemen. He was eight months old when Bill Nauman bought him. Bill, only a high school boy at the time, had been to a sale at the Dear Ranch, and the horse he wanted had sold for more money than he had. So, after the sale when Mr. Anderson mentioned the gray colt, priced at $95, Bill became interested. He liked Stormy, and bought him.

Stormy Boy is by Red Colonel, a horse bred by Bryan Packard of Colorado Springs. Red Colonel's sire was Reno's Golden Chief, and his dam was Red Squaw, both of these being J. J. Wiescamp-bred horses. Stormy's dam was a grade mare called Peggy, hence Stormy's Appendix standing in AQHA.

Bill Nauman broke and trained Stormy himself. His first rodeo on the gray horse was the high school rodeo at Deer Lodge, Montana, in 1954. Up to this time, Bill had roped on Stormy quite a lot, but had never bulldogged from him. He was entered in the bareback riding, breaking away roping and tie-down roping at this rodeo upon arriving at Deer Lodge, found they had too many ropers, so he had to draw out of one roping event. However, he was able to enter another event, so he chose bulldogging. Just before the rodeo he was warming Stormy up in the infield, and leaned over like he would in getting down on a steer. Bill said "Stormy jumped about 20 feet to the left and I sure got down!" He didn't place in the dogging that day either, but a lot of practice overcame Stormy's fear of someone hanging on his side.

Bill started college rodeoing with Stormy in 1956 at Montana State University. He mounted nearly all the rodeo team in the dogging the next three years. In 1958, Junior Small of Kirby, was the NIRA champion bulldogger, using Stormy all season. The following year,

Bill Nauman won the Rocky Mountain Region bulldogging, was third in calf roping, and third in ribbon roping on Stormy. This pair finished third in the Nation for the National Intercollegiate Rodeo Association that year also.

Bill said he has won or placed in the roping and dogging at nearly all major RCA rodeos in Montana and some in Canada, riding Stormy Boy. He generally mounts a few of the cowboys on Stormy, and many times his mount money more than pays the Naumans' way on the road.

Several years ago Bill entered Stormy in a few AQHA approved shows, and won the championship at Great Falls twice. In 1960 he was the Montana State Champion Rope Horse for the year. However, not until 1967 did Nauman's decide to go all out for Quarter Horse shows with their fine gray horse. At this time he was 17 years of age.

Bill Nauman and Nona Brown first met in 1954, and were married in 1958. Nona is a daughter of well-known horseman Edgar Brown of Helena, and the whole family are riders and contestants. Nona is a barrel racer, and recently was president of the Montana Barrel Racers Association. They have two sons, Jeff, five, and Mike, seven.

Nauman's are getting started in the Quarter Horse breeding business, along with their cattle, and have five good broodmares and a stallion, Han-Leo-Bert by Leo Hancock, and out of Minnie Bert. His dam was a barrel racing and cutting mare, and his sire, Leo Hancock, is a well-known working horse sire. Bill and Nona have run barrels on Han-Leo-Bert, cut cows on him, and now Bill is steer roping on him. They believe in all-around using horses, and this stallion is filling the bill in all ways.

Beginning the Montana Quarter Horse Show circuit is Winter Fair in Bozeman, in early February. This year Stormy and Bill Nauman began their contesting at Bozeman, winning second in both calf roping and heeling in the steer roping. Next they went to Glendive, where Stormy placed fifth at halter, second in calf roping, third in heeling, and first in senior reining. He also was the all-around performance champion.

At Polson on June 7, Bill and Stormy won fourth in the calf roping, second in the senior reining, and they won both the heeling and western riding. The following Sunday at the Big Sky show at Dear's near Simms, they again won the western riding, heeling, calf roping, and second in senior reining. Stormy was all-around champion performance horse here also.

Forsyth brought another pair of wins, in calf roping and senior reining. And then to Choteau early in July, where they took home first place honors in calf roping, second in senior reining and second in the working cow horse class, as well as a sixth in the aged gelding halter class, with 13 horses entered. But, the highlight of the Choteau show was none of these wins. Little five-year-old Jeff showed Stormy Boy in the western pleasure for children under 14 years of age, and won! Never were the stars brighter in a little boy's eyes as he accepted the blue ribbon and rode back to where his mother, father and older brother waited, beaming with pride. Nona said later that Stormy Boy never made a wrong move in this class, that he was taking care of Jeff all the way, and seemed to realize his responsibilities.

Brother Mike has ridden Stormy Boy in western pleasure twice, placing both times, but this was Jeff's first time to compete.

Following the Choteau show came the big one in Missoula. Stormy Boy won the all-around championship honors in performance by winning the heeling, second in senior reining and third in calf roping.

At the State Fair Quarter Horse Show in Great Falls the first of August, Bill and Stormy were very much in evidence with another all-around championship, placing and winning in three events again.

As the short show season in Montana nears the end, it is almost a sure bet the gray horse from Augusta will be the high-point performance horse of the year.

And so old Stormy Boy, the 17-year-old horse that carried Bill Nauman to many wins in his high school and college rodeo days continues his good work in RCA rodeos and now in AQHA shows. A good, honest, all-around horse that never fails to do his best… once they get him caught!

SUNDAY GLORY

March 1966

Perhaps one of the top rope horses of all times, and surely one of the greatest living today, is owned by George Richmond, Remuda Training Stable, Hayden Lake, Idaho. Sunday Glory is his name, and a fitting name at that, for Sunday has brought a lot of glory (and not only on Sundays) to his owner the years he has been in the arena.

He has brought a lot of bruises, too, but George went along with this because the horse had so much potential and George had so much hope for him. It took a long time for the horse to get to the point where he wouldn't bog his head and buck, but all this time he was placing at a lot of ropings, too.

George Richmond is a well-known rodeo cowboy and announcer, and his training stable at Hayden Lake is buzzing with activity and good horses. The pet of the stable, of course, is Sunday Glory.

Sunday was foaled in 1947 on the ranch of Pierce Rhodes, Sedona, Arizona. His sire was Glory by El Rey by Sykes by Peter McCue, and his dam was a double-bred Possum mare. Glory's dam was a Ben Hur mare. As soon as George saw this colt as a long two-year-old, he wanted him.

At the time, George was working for Charles A. Ward, Camp Verde, Arizona, training horses. The Rhodes ranch was nearby, and Pierce invited George over to use his arena whenever he wished, and he let him ride Sunday when he wanted, also.

The colt was green at the time, and George would run calves and steers on him for practice and eventually began to rope slow calves on him. Sunday seemed to have more natural ability as a rope horse than any George has ever ridden, and he tried to get Pierce to put a price on him. Apparently Pierce had the same idea, for he said he planned to keep Sunday for himself.

In the fall of 1951, George received a letter from Pierce saying he had decided to sell the sorrel colt, and he priced him at $500. George immediately sent him $100 to hold Sunday but did not get to Arizona to pick him up until July 1952. The Richmonds had bought a small ranch at Park City, Montana, the fall before, and were unable to get away.

George was roping at Ogden and Salt Lake City Rodeos in July 1952, and since he had drawn up for the latter part of the first rodeo, decided to spend his extra time in going to Sedona to pick up the new horse.

He had not been able to notify Pierce of his coming, so there was nobody at home when he arrived. (Later he found out that Pierce was off at a big team roping someplace.) George hadn't seen Sunday since the winter he was a coming three-year-old, and now he was past five, but he knew the horse and immediately when he found him in a pasture close by with a bunch of other horses. Sunday was big and fat and had really filled out a lot. And he liked his home so well that it was quite a job to get him loaded in the trailer! But after a struggle, the end gate was fastened, note left for Pierce, and George headed back for Ogden, proud as he could be of his new rope-horse, he hoped.

Arriving at Ogden rodeo grounds, he decided to saddle Sunday and show him off to his cowboy friends. Sunday had a big hump in his back and tried to buck, and George arrived at the conclusion that this horse hadn't been used very much since he last rode him. He was still pretty green for his age, and that thick fat wasn't there for nothing!

But a lot of cowboying back home on the ranch in Montana took some of the buck out of Sunday. Not all of it though, for anytime he wanted to he could unload his pack, and he knew it. A powerful horse for his size, and quick, though not too big, it wasn't much of a problem for him. But it was for his owner and rider, because George wanted to make a top roping horse of this sorrel, and he aimed to do it or else!

With a lot of hard rides, soon George was roping on him, and the horse again showed his natural ability as a calf horse.

The following spring, Sunday saw his first rodeo as a contest horse at Rigby, Idaho. There were over 40 ropers at this two-day rodeo, and the cowboys only got one calf. Dean Oliver, later to become many times Champion, won the roping, and George won second on this new horse of his. Maybe he should have let it go at that, but after the rodeo was over, as cowboys will do, George offered to rope one of the extra calves just for practice. He was told, "Sure, if you will hurry up." So George hurried. In face he hurried so much that he rode right into the box without tightening his cinch. The calf was a fast little Brahma, and it wasn't but a few jumps out of the box that Sunday's cattle shifted a little. Sunday came undone, and George says, "For some reason I just kept swinging my rope. That didn't last long though, and I'd probably have gone back into orbit if I hadn't had hold of that rope to bring me back down!"

The next night was the beginning of a three-performance rodeo at Blackfoot, Idaho. It was a two-calf average, and George got off to a real good start by winning the first go-round. The next go-round, he was up after the rodeo, and it was a really chilly night. Apparently he didn't warm his horse up enough, for Sunday blew up and bucked him off going to the calf. Right then and there, George decided this was getting to be too much of a habit, so he simply took Sunday back to the ranch and more hard work and wet saddle blankets.

And so it went. Up to the time Sunday was thirteen years old, in 1960, none of the cowboys had any luck riding him, and no one was anxious to rope on him, for word got around that George was putting up a bucking horse ride in conjunction with his calf roping. Several had tried Sunday, but he'd buck every time anyone else got on him, so they wanted no part of him. George wasn't about to give up on the sorrel horse, in spite of biting the dust now and then, for Sunday's good traits far outweighed the bad, and they were placing often enough that George was encouraged.

He laughs when he tells this story: "At Billings in 1958 I think it was, I rode up along the outside of the arena fence to watch the bareback riding. I was sitting on Sunday, relaxing and enjoying the show, when a bareback horse bucked right up to the fence and threw his rider over the fence in front of us. Well, that touched ol' Sunday off. He sheered and snorted and let me have it. I could see the top of the grandstand and the ferris wheel before I came down, and of course everyone in the grandstand had been watching this bareback horse which trigged the explosion, so they saw it all. They roared of course, and Oral Zumwalt, the rodeo producer, came over. He wasn't concerned about me plowing up the infield grass with my head; he wanted to hire my act for the balance of the season!"

Then he adds, "But come to think of it, I believe I won the roping there that year."

Besides placing at most of the smaller rodeos they worked, George and Sunday won a second at Denver in the average of 1958, and third in the average in 1960, which was no small accomplishment.

In the spring of 1960, George was busy moving to his present location at Hayden Lake, and didn't get much riding done. However, the rest seemed to agree with Sunday, for he worked like a professional at the Edmonton, Alberta rodeo in May, his first contest since Denver, and George won the roping there.

The top cowboys never hesitated to take a seat on Sunday Glory once he settled down, and they felt confident in winning or placing on him. If for any reason they were contesting without their own horses and Sunday was available, they felt safe in asking George to mount them, and George felt equally safe in offering his horse to a good cowboy, for a fourth of their winnings belonged to him as owner of the rope horse.

In 1960, George and Sunday went to Lethbridge, Alberta. This was the week before the Calgary Stampede, and there were a lot of American cowboys there, en route to the Stampede. Among these was Dale Smith. Salinas followed Calgary, so Dale had left his fine rope horse Poker Chip Peake in California, planning on flying back to Salinas from Calgary. He asked to ride Sunday at Letherbridge, George had this to say about the occasion: "Dale rides a rope horse as good or better than anyone in rodeo, so I figured they'd get along okay, which proved to be correct. Due to the big entry list, everyone was to get one calf, and then the eight high men out of that go-round would rope a final calf. Dale tied his first calf in 10 seconds flat, but was penalized an extra ten seconds for jerking the calf down, in accordance with Canadian rules at that time. Otherwise he would easily have won the go-round."

The next day there was a one-day rodeo at Coleman, Alberta, with what George terms one of the toughest ropings he has ever seen. Besides roping, George was announcing this rodeo. Again there was a long list of ropers, mostly Americans. They were using fast little whiteface calves that had been used once previously, and were roping over a fifteen-foot score with a deep box. Dale Smith roped on Sunday again and tied his calf in the most unbelievable time of :08.8 seconds. George says, "This was the fastest calf I've ever seen tied in competition. And if my memory serves me correctly, Jim Bob Altizer was :09.5; Dean Oliver, :09.8; and Bob Ragsdale and Grady Allen split fourth with :10 flat. This under Canadian rules, too! We went on to Calgary from there, and Dale won the first go-round and the average riding Sunday."

A game, great-hearted horse, Sunday performed at these three rodeos with an injured tendon in his left from ankle. This injury occurred just before Lethbridge, and although George ran cold water on it day and night and tried "everyone's favorite remedy," his horse was getting lamer all the time. When Dale and George roped their last calves at Calgary, Sunday sat back on three legs and held the lame leg out stiff in front of him while working the rope. George said, "I gave him a well-deserved rest and a chance to heal up after Calgary. It sure proved what a terrific heart that ol' pony has."

In 1961 the Diamond Spur rodeo at Spokane and Calgary conflicted. Spokane was but a few miles from Hayden Lake, so George naturally stayed close to home. However, a lot of the good cowboys were flying to Spokane from Calgary, working both rodeos. Naturally they were looking for a good horse to ride at Spokane. Doug McLaughlin, Bill Murray, Rob Wiley and George Richmond all rode Sunday Glory. Murray won two second day-monies and first in the average, and George placed on both his claves and won third in the average.

Later that same season, Bob Wiley and Mark Shricker flew to the Omak, Washington rodeo from Caldwell, Idaho, and both asked to be mounted on Sunday. Wiley won both go-rounds and the average; Shricker placed in the go-rounds and won second in the average; and George won fourth in the average.

Jack McSpadden rode Sunday at Newport, Washington, and won the roping there. That fall at the Pendleton Roundup, Don McLaughlin rode him on his second calf and won a third day money.

Just a short time before the National Finals that year, George received a call from Bob Wiley in California saying he needed a horse to ride, and he wanted to lease or buy Sunday. George says, "I promised Sunday at Calgary, when he worked like he did, that I'd never sell him. But I knew Bob would take care of him, so agreed to lease the horse to him for the Finals and the big winter and spring rodeos. I got him back right after Phoenix, which was just right to begin our rodeo season up here in the Northwest."

In 1962, the Spokane Quarter Horse Show started having youth classes along with their performance and halter events. George's son Lee was but eleven-years-old at the time, a slim little fellow, but already an excellent rider for his age. George was training several horses about that time, at this particular time was committed to show one of them in senior reining. So Lee showed Sunday Glory against mostly adults. When it came time for Lee and Sunday to perform, George rode over and told him, "You'd better turn ol' Sunday loose!" There had been some real good performances up until then. So turn him loose Lee did, and when the dust settled, judge Hugh Bennett and young Lee had matching smiles, for the team of Lee and Sunday was judged winner of the senior bit reining! Lee also won the youth reining, roping, and was third in the western pleasure.

Actually, about the only time Sunday competes in Quarter Horse shows is when the show is in conjunction with a rodeo. However, one time worthy of a special mention was his trip to the Walla Walla Winter Show in 1962. George had entered Sunday in three events, senior reining, rope horse class, and working cow horse class; he won them all. He was the Champion Working Horse of this show.

IN 1963, four top ropers were riding Sunday at Calgary: Dale Smith, Bob Wiley, Mel Potter, and George Richmond. Dale won the first go-round and George won third; Wiley won the next second go-round in :13 flat; Dale was second with :13.1 and Mel was third in :13.2. The sixteen high men of the two go-rounds roped a final calf, and all four of the ropers had qualified. Mel had left however, after roping his second calf, thinking he had failed to qualify for the final run. Dale won the average and Wiley was second. This was the year Sunday Glory set a record for the total amount of money earned on one rope horse at one rodeo...$8,369! Another $25 was awarded to best rope horse, which naturally went to Sunday.

At Pendleton in 1963, a new event for the Roundup was introduced; this was the working cowhorse event, with a $1500 purse plus #75 entry fee. Horses from five states competed that year, each working four go-rounds. And Sunday Glory was the winner. So George points with pride to the huge silver trophy, valued at $1500, which has his and Sunday's names engraved on it. True enough, this trophy must be won three times for permanent possession, but it is still quite an honor to have even one log on it. A prize like this isn't given to a horse and rider for nothing, and it was for sure that George and Sunday earned this one!

And to top it off, at this same rodeo, Dale Smith and Bob Wiley were both roping calves on Sunday, and Dale won the average on him.

In 1964, Sunday gave a repeat performance at Calgary, again winning the prize for the best rope horse. Dale Smith and Bob Wiley were again riding him and placed in the roping. George won third in the average.

Pendleton that year wasn't quite so lucky. Dale tied his calf in :10.8, but the calf got up before the :06 second waiting period, resulting in no time. George and Sunday were in the lead in the working cow horse class, but a sulky cow that refused to budge, set them back so they split third and fourth in the average. They made the ten high, going into the finals in the roping, but failed to place in the average.

At Edmonton in 1965, George won the senior reining and rope horse class. At Calgary that year, five ropers rode Sunday. All placed in the day monies, and Lee Farris won the average.

The day after Calgary ended, George noticed Sunday was favoring a hind ankle. Apparently he had sprained it working in the deep mud in the arena the day before. However, a short rest helped him.

Later at Medicine Hat, George tied a calf in :10.5, to win the second go-round. He tied a wild, squirmy little calf at Letherbridge in :13.2. Sunday was working perfectly, although after each run his ankle would bother him. According to George, "That's characteristic of the ol' pony. He's got so much courage he'll work every time even if he's sore or hurting. The ankle was getting progressively worse, so I brought him home and laid him up for the balance of the season. He's fat and frisky now and apparently as sound as ever. Although he'll be nineteen in the spring, as near as I could tell this year, until he was injured, he hadn't slowed up at all and was real sharp, so I'm looking forward to making more runs on him at some of the big rodeos in 1966."

Had George traveled steady, who knows, perhaps he and Sunday Glory might have been World's Champion roping team. But George, like many of the rodeo people, has his home and business to manage, and he just travels when he's able to get away for a few days.

He is turning out some good working horses and rope horses at Remuda Training Stable, but it is doubtful if he will ever have another to equal the great little Sunday Glory.

JOE HUT

January 1966

A handsome bay horse bounded from the box, came to a sliding, square stop when the roper caught his calf and went on to work the rope like the true champion he was.

Somebody said, "Say, what is that little bay horse?"

"That horse?" came the answer. "Why, that's Joe. 'Most everybody knows Joe!"

Maybe at that time, years ago, it was stretching things a little, but now, after about 13 years of work, and most of it in and around arenas, few in the rodeo world, young or old, have to ask "Who is Joe?" For he is one of the best-known horses in the business today. Unless you are an absolute newcomer to the rodeo, at one time or another you have probably witnessed a performance where Joe was working in one event or another.

This hard-working horse was foaled in 1947 on the well-known Carlsbad, New Mexico ranch of Elmer Hepler. His registered name is Joe Hut, and he is by Little Joe the Wrangler P-774 by Joe Hancock P-455. His dam was Hut Sut P-17,658 by Valentine Hepler by Lone Star. Hut Sut was out of the mare Patsy Clegg by Albert by Hickory Bill.

Little Joe the Wrangler's dam was Hepler's Goldie P-7725 by the Thoroughbred horse Madder Music. So here is a combination of some of the best old-time breeding, plus just enough Thoroughbred to make things interesting.

Joe's record is actually stranger than fiction, for it is unbelievable that one horse could perform so well at so many different jobs and do each chore with equal ease and success.

To begin with, he spent a rather uneventful life at his New Mexico home, along with other colts his age. But one thing about Joe's early life stood out from the rest. When he was two, he got too close to a cranky rattlesnake and was bitten on the right side of his neck. Even today he carries the scar, and anything sounding even remotely like a rattlesnake will scare the wits out of him.

Joe wasn't broke to ride until he was four, and at that time he didn't act like he would ever learn anything. Oral Zumwalt brought him up from Heplers and tried to make a calf roping horse of him. Joe worked the rope right from the start, doing as near a perfect job as any green horse could. But he wouldn't run. Oral knew he had run in him, but it just took time to bring it out. He went on using the horse around the ranch. At the time, Oral and Bud Lake had the KO Rodeo Company, with headquarters up Miller Creek, out of Missoula, Montana, and here it was that Joe got most of his early education.

Bill Lawrence, who was rodeoing then, lived at Augusta, Montana and one day he came over to Missoula while Oral was working Joe, getting ready for a big roping. Anyone who knew Oral knew he was a perfectionist, and he was mighty particular about the way his horses worked. This was proven time after time in the arena, where Oral was the many-times winner of roping and bulldogging contests at all the major rodeos in this country and Canada. He was a good hand, and he was always well-mounted. That is a combination pretty hard to beat.

This particular time Oral told Bill he wasn't having too much luck in getting Joe to run like he figured his horse could. So Bill made a deal to take Joe Hunt back to Augusta, where he was readying a string of relay horses for a fair and race meet. After a couple weeks ponying race horses, Joe finally got the idea it was fun to extend himself and outrun those other horses, and he was "off to the races!"

Bill roped calves on him some at the end of his two weeks' session with ponying, and he would catch a calf so fast it was hard for Bill to get his rope swinging.

From then on, between Bill, Oral and Joe, they could always count on a big share of the pay-off money. Joe was one of Oral's favorite mounts of all the many good horses he rode, and he refused many an offer on the horse, stating that Joe was worth more than mere money.

It would be impossible to even estimate the number of miles Joe Hut has traveled to and from rodeos, fairs, and race meets. For years he has been on the road constantly, and he was at home whenever his grain bucket was, right from the start. He travels well and doesn't gaunt up like a lot of horses do. But then Joe isn't nervous or high-strung, and he pretty well takes care of himself in that respect. Getting him ready to run or work isn't much of a problem, whether in pasture or at the manger at home. Just put your saddle on him and go, for it seems that Joe just was "born ready."

Often Oral would mount cowboys on Joe in rodeos, and Joe always did his best. You could actually see the anger that he felt if his rider had to take two loops to catch a calf, or if the dogger he was hazing for failed to jump for his steer. Joe would lay back his ears and shake his head. He knows how it is done, and it is too bad old Joe couldn't talk for he sure could educate a lot of young cowboys. As it was, Joe's "I'll do it my way and you can ride along" attitude carried many a young newcomer to the pay window. Joe did his best, providing they gave him half a chance.

The KO Rodeo was a busy concern for several years, and Joe was one of the main performers, both in the arena and around the ranch. Just an average day for this horse could begin at 4:30 a.m. (for Oral was noted as an early riser) when they started to work stock, sorting and cutting in the corrals to get ready to load out another rodeo. Joe is an excellent horse for this type of work, alert and willing, cutting horses and cattle into different pens and corrals. Then, with the stock loaded and hauled to the rodeo grounds, Joe would be used to run calves and steers. Then he would be readied for the grand entry. Sometimes he was even used as a pickup horse for hazing stock from the arena. He was always in the roping and dogging, and was very popular hazing horse, usually ridden by Oral Zumwalt or Bill Lawrence.

As the years went by, Joe seemed to stand still as far as age and contain went. He performed consistently year after year, and his great courage has made him a lasting impression on all who know him. He has the respect of the cowboys, whether they are competing on him or against him.

During all this time, Joe was making a name for himself in short races, from 450 yards to just across the arena. He came out of the box like a shot, and he came from the starting gate just the same way. He wasn't a rangy or racey-built horse, yet in his day Joe showed his little heels to many a good racing Quarter Horse and Thoroughbred alike.

Oral and Bill, and Bill's wife Mikell (Mike,) were interested in racing horses, and the urge to try Joe whenever possible "overcame good sense," as Mike puts it. "Once at Hamilton Fair and Rodeo, Oral met me on the race track when I was leading Joe back after a race, with a stock saddle over his shoulder. We switched from the jockey saddle to the stock saddle, and while I went to collect the old horse's check for winning the race, Oral rode into the arena to haze a few steers."

At Kalispell one year, the roping and dogging was all won on Joe, as well as the quarter-mile race.

Joe was never actually trained for racing, but he could out-break all but the best at the gate. He would always walk in quietly, stand with his nose in the V of the gate, and wait patiently with only his ears moving. It seemed to be the vibration he was waiting for, and if it happened to be a slow gate, Joe was already on his way, and the Jockey had better take care of his knees!

Joe was tough. Once when Bill was hauling him and Oral's stallion to the College Rodeo in Bozeman, somehow the stallion got his head loose and spent his time for the entire distance chewing on poor Joe's neck. Unknown to Bill, the horse's neck was mangled considerably, requiring the care of a veterinarian in Bozeman. And all that time Joe never fought back nor moved enough for Bill to realize through the movement of the trailer that anything was wrong. When the vet sewed him up, old Joe didn't move.

Many times Oral said it was a shame Joe was ever gelded, for if he had been left entire and could pass on his characteristics to his get, what a great old sire he would have been!

In the early summer of 1962, Oral Zumwalt passed away, the victim of a heart attack at the Big Timber rodeo. Living the life he loved best, the life of rodeo, he was flanking a buckling horse when the end came. So the burden of operating the KO Rodeo went to Bill, who by that time owned an interest in the company.

When Mrs. Zumwalt decided to sell the outfit, Bill's first thoughts were of Old Joe. The bond between Bill and Joe had grown through the years, and the thought of parting with that bay horse was just too much for Bill. So he and Mrs. Zumwalt got their heads together, and when their deal was settled, one-third interest in KO Rodeo Company belonged to Mrs. Zumwalt, a straight-across trade. Bill valued that bay horse mighty highly!

Joe was the ripe old age of 15 at the time, and Bill had this to say: "It's a helluva price to pay for the old guy, but even if he never sees another calf, he's won me enough to not owe me anything now."

The following spring, Joe was the one kick and bucking the highest when rodeo time came along, and when Bill and Mike were loading their horses for the first trip, Joe hung his head over the gate and nickered until they pulled out. His place was in the arena, and he couldn't bear to give up the starring role to a newcomer.

Well, Joe is 19 this year, and you name anything from shooting a deer off his back, to rodeoing, and even baby-sitting for the Lawrence's three little children, and Joe has done it.

He is no slouch at team roping, working both as a heading and heeling horse, and recent added polo to the list of his achievements. The only thing he has flatly refused to do is barrel race. Mike tried him at that event, and he just didn't have the heart for it. There were no cattle, horses or cowboys to compete against or show off to, so barrel racing wasn't for Old Joe.

Bill has had several horses in training and usually has a new one riding in one side of his trailer. But even today when the competition is tough and the stakes are high, he catches Joe because, as Mike says, there is nothing tougher over the long average than an old rodeo hand mounted on an old rodeo horse.

Take an arena, any arena, fill it with cowboys, horses, cattle, and confusion, and Joe is right at home. A little slower perhaps at age 19, maybe a little shorter-winded, but with that old fire and will still burning high in his great heart. His love of the arena will be with him as long as he can follow a calf, for Old Joe Hut is a real campaigner and he will be to the end.

And the end will come in time, but many, many people will never forget that wonderful bay gelding that carried so many cowboys to the pay window, always doing his honest best, helping the newcomers and working with the top hands.

When rodeo folks gather and discuss horses, some one is bound to say, "Do you remember Old Joe, Oral Zumwalt and Bill Lawrence's bay horse? Did you see him up at …?" … and so on and on. For Joe will remain a legend to rodeo people even after his days are long past. Joe, with his unusual intelligence, knows rodeo almost as well as the cowboys themselves.

SERGEANT GILL

October 1966

Many years have passed since this young fellow rode mule-back. Many horses have been ridden, many calves have been roped, and many changes have been made in his life. Now the little boy is the well-known rancher and rodeo cowboy Bob Lytle of Santa Rita, Montana. Maybe Bob's favorite mount at one time was a mule, but today he is as well-mounted as any cowboy in the business.

Bob Lytle came by his cowboying honestly. His father, Matt Lytle, used to do rodeo, as did his uncle Floyd Peters. So between the two of them, they groomed Bob for a future winner. Matt finished the horses, and Floyd taught him to rope and tie. Bob rodeoed when he was in high school in 1953. Then, three years later he attended the Toots Mansfield Roping School for some time. The following spring,

Uncle Floyd took him to Edmonton, Alberta where he placed in two go-rounds and won a fourth in the average. Quite an accomplishment for this young calf roper, and it certainly gave his confidence a boost.

Meantime, Bob was thinking of more important things than rodeo. He had met a girl who was later to become his wife. Then he went to the Willard Combs ranch in Oklahoma, broke his leg bulldogging, and came back home. He tells it this way: "She proposed to me, and in the fall of 1958 we were married." Lorna comes from Craig, Montana, a little town near Great Falls. She is a good hand with a horse, and as do a lot of cowboys' wives, she barrel races.

Jay Bob Lytle came along in November of 1959, and he has been livening things up ever since. At the age of six, he is already on the road to becoming a calf roper. Everything that can climb goes up a post when young Jay Bob appears with his rope. He lives and thinks cowboys and calf roping, and the way this youngster is going, he might well be a World's Champion by 1980! Seldom seen without a rope in his hand, Jay Bob is after everything from chickens to calves at home, and the last two years he has been roping Shetland pony colts at the Little Buckaroo Rodeo at the Missoula County Fair. While there, he can be seen back of the miniature chutes, in all seriousness, coaching the little fellows (and girls) about his size, on the proper way to hold their ropes and how to catch whatever they are aiming for.

Bob Lytle is proud of his good sorrel rope horse, Sergeant Gill, P-40,689, and as well he may be, for this horse has carried him to top honors in rodeo.

Sarge, as he is called, was foaled in May 1950, which made him 16 years old this year. When a using horse reaches this age, he is past his prime, and this is of no little concern to Bob because it is not easy to replace a faithful horse. And Sarge gets a lot of extra care. He is as sound as can be and appears to be ready for several more good years in the arena.

Bred by the Gill Cattle Company, Sarge's sire was My Texas Dandy, Jr. by My Texas Dandy, and his dam was Gill Cattle Co. Mare #35, a daughter of Bear Hug. He comes by his working ability naturally. With good schooling and a way with cattle, Sergeant Gill just couldn't miss! He is a big, stout horse, well-suited to Bob, for this roper is well over six feet tall. It is astonishing how much grace and speed these big, husky ropers can muster when competing and Sarge is a match for any speedy roper. He is a smoothing working horse and has a terrific stop.

Bob says Sarge has no bad habits and is thoroughly dependable. He always works the same. You can count on him, and if you do your part, you can be sure the big sorrel horse will do his. So all Bob has to do is worry about his own abilities; he hasn't the additional worry of a contrary or undependable mount. A very capable roper, Bob has shown his prowess with a rope since 1955 when he won his first contest at a rodeo in Glacier Park. From that time on, he has won and place at many of the major rodeos across the country. He is unable to rodeo full time because of his ranching interest, so he does miss a lot of contests. But whenever he goes, they know big Bob Lyle was there, and he generally packs home a share of the prize money.

Sarge has a bold, sure way of running to a calf. He stands quietly in the box, full of anticipation, waiting for just the right word or motion to put him into action. He knows what it's all about, and he isn't about to make any mistakes. He didn't learn all this overnight however. It takes months and months of hard training to achieve perfection in any kind of using horse, and Sarge's early training was no exception. But to begin with, he had the qualifications to make a top horse and the right kind of training.

Herb Doenz of Big Horn, Wyoming, trained Sarge and rodeoed on him for several years. Bob had ridden him at Fort Worth in 1958 and immediately took a liking to the horse. Most of these good rope horses are hard to buy, but Bob got the job done at the Denver Stock Show in 1959. Sarge isn't strictly a calf roping horse either. Bob uses him as a general ranch using horse, for a hazing and team roping horse, and for wild cow milking contests. Bob is a calf roper mainly, but he enters bulldogging, team roping, cow milking, and now and then hazes for another 'doggers.

While Herb owned him, Sarge won Grand Champion Gelding honors at the Quarter Horse show in Forsyth, Montana. This was in 1957. He also has been campaigned some by Bob in registered roping and reining and has earned his Register of Merit in both events. Usually this pair is too busy rodeoing to work Quarter Horse shows, but at the Great Falls show in both 1963 and 1965, they won the registered roping.

Traveling never bothers Sarge. He works the same indoors or out, and Bob proudly says, "The thing about Sarge is that he is honest, easy to score, and runs to cattle true."

He pretty well takes care of himself and has been crippled only once since Bob owned him. This happened in the roping finals at the Calgary Stampede last year. The arena was a sea of mud, and Sarge over-reached, cutting himself. He was laid up three weeks as a result of his injury.

The Lytles got quite a scare a couple of years ago when they stopped to visit Lorna's family at Lincoln, Montana. Bob unloaded his horse, put him in the next corral and fed him, and went in to eat breakfast. When he came out to load his horse for the trip homeward, the horse was gone! Bob hunted for Sarge for over two weeks and had friends and neighbors doing the same. They even had an airplane out looking for him.

They had given up ever locating the horse, when six weeks later, a friend of Bob's from Augusta, Doc Alt, called and told him to come get his horse. Where did he find him? Right back in the corral from where he disappeared! It was thought that someone had "borrowed" him to take on a hunting trip. Well, if he did the job as well as he works for Bob, he probably earned his keep. He was none the worse for his adventure, whatever it may have been.

Once Bob and Sarge got to rodeoing together, they made quite a team, and in 1958 at Denver, Bob won a second behind Glen Franklin, to the tune of nearly $700. At Edmonton, Alberta, in 1961 they won the roping, $800 and a beautiful trophy horse blanket. They won a second at Lewiston, Idaho, in 1961, won the average at Medicine Hat, Alberta, that same year, and at Havre, Montana, in 1963 Bob tied two calves in :23.1 to win the average. In Swift Current, Saskatchewan, they won the roping in 1963, and a beautiful trophy saddle, which Bob in turn gave to his dad in appreciation for all the help given to further his rodeo career.

Sometimes, in fact more often than not nowadays, a cowboy will make several rodeos in a week, if they aren't too far apart. In 1962 Bob won fifth in the average at Calgary and won the short go-round. The next day he won second in the team roping at Conrad, Montana, with his father as his partner. Then immediately afterwards he won the first go-round in the roping, second in the second ground and first in the average at Shelby, Montana. He was going back and forth from Shelby to Medicine Hat, and he won a third in the average at The Hat. Bob and Sarge won both the July and October ropings and Shaunavan, Saskatchewan, in 1963. At Brooks, Alberta, they split first and second with Jim Gladstone with a good time of :10.5. Bob's share of this purse amounted to $172.50.

Bob has won Kalispell, Montana twice, riding Sarge; he won Belt, the Great Falls State Fair, Shelby, Deer Lodge, and Lewiston, Montana and Edmonton, Alberta. He rodeos considerably in Canada, since it is handier to his northern Montana location.

In 1964 Bob and Sarge won in Kalispell and Big Sandy, Montana, Regina, Saskatchewan, and Wainright, Alberta. At Yakima, Washington, they won a go-round and placed second in the average.

In the Saskatchewan-Manitoba annual standings in 1964, Bob was in fifth place.

In the rodeo program at Ellensburg, Washington, one of the larger rodeos in the country, Bob and Sarge had taken a jackpot sponsored by the Silver Buckle Rodeo, in Polson, Montana. In spite of an injured knee which gives him a considerable amount of trouble, Bob has put the state of Montana on the map as far as calf roping is concerned. Much of this credit he gives to Sarge. In Calgary in 1965, this pair won nearly a thousand dollars by placing second in the first go-round in the calf roping. Sarge won over $3600 in 1965, ridden by Bob and Herb Doen.

So, it has been a busy life for this young cowboy who used to ride a mule back. And it has also been a busy life for the big sorrel gelding that wears the Arrowhead brand of the Gill Cattle Company.

NOCHES DRIFTER

September 1966

Noches Drifter

Canada has always had a very lively interest in horses. Jumping is one of their main events in the horse field, and it is amazing to see even the small children taking the jumps like veterans, some on large ponies, but many of them on average-size saddle horses.

Breeds of jumpers vary, although Thoroughbreds have been the favorite for this sport. Some horsemen claim the straight Thoroughbred is a little too fine-boned, and perhaps a bit too excitable, so they may go more to a cross-bred horse. Pinto, Palominos, Appaloosas... any color may be seen in these crossbreds, and any one of them may be a very able horse.

Since the American Quarter Horse Association has approved a jumping class, the Quarter Horse is coming to the front in a hurry.

They are a sturdier breed, quieter in temperament, and they seem to accept the jumps very well.

Up in Edmonton, Alberta, Johanna Laskin and her fine black mare, Noches Drifter have done a great deal to further the advancement of the jumping Quarter Horse in Canada.

Truly, a prime example of the versatility of our Quarter Horse, Noches has a record of many achievements, and she has a great future in store for herself. Bred by Edward Smith, San Rafael, California, she is eight years old, and was sired by Booger H by King and out of the mare Coal Bin by Driftwood. When she was a two-year-old, Don Dodge thought she should be a good cutting prospect, so he bought her and moved her to his training stables at Sacramento, where her cutting training was begun. This was where she was seen by Bill Collins, another top hand in Western riding, cutting and roping. Bill is from Canada and has use quite a name for himself in the line of horse training, and he knows a good one when he sees it.

He took Notes Drifter back to Canada with him and put her in extensive cutting training. She was winning some novice classes, but she just didn't seem to want to put forth as much effort as a top cutting horse should. However, Bill continued to ride her, and she was getting some attention from by-standers by this time. Soon Johann Laskin discovered her, liked her, and bought her from Bill. She began showing the mare in western pleasure classes and did very well.

Bill was still working with her, and soon Johann was winning western riding classes as well.

In the fall of 1964, Drifter's future as a jumping horse was assured, when Johann entered her in a trail horse class. One of the obstacles was a brush fence, and the black mare took this one best of all. Johann says, "I liked the way she hunted into it, ears well forward, and she folded her legs well, so I got the idea I should try to take some jumping lessons on her." The idea then was to finish the mare for her nine-year-old son Mark to compete on. Mark is riding a good little pony that is 13-1 hands, and he is advancing to the stage where he can use a larger horse.

So, Johann showed Drifter to Cheryl Forst, an outstanding jumping horse rider and trainer. Cheryl thought the mare showed promise. This young lady had taken her English riding training in Ireland as well as from Gene Lewis in Sacramento. She is giving instructions to others now.

Cheryl was going back to California to further her training in English riding and jumping with Gene Lewis so Johann asked her to take Drifter along. So it was back to the Don Dodge Stables for Drifter, since Gene is training there.

Johann joined them in February on her vacation, and the next month they all returned to Canada, including the mare.

Don Dodge had been very impressed with her jumping ability, and along with some training in western riding, he gave her a good start in jumping training. After about a month's work, his little daughter Cathy showed Drifter in a junior show and made an excellent showing. She won second in open western pleasure; she won the Quarter Horse western pleasure and the open hunter hack. Then in the children's working hunter class where they had three-foot jumps, she placed fifth. In the green jumper class she placed second. This was plenty of encouragement for anyone, and Johann took her mare back to Edmonton with stars in her eyes!

In 1965 this pair won most of the Quarter Horse jumping classes they entered. They also placed several times in the first-year green hunter classes.

She is only 15-1 hands tall, but this black mare was becoming more and more the horse to watch. Although the judges generally prefer the 16 to 17 hand horses for open hunters, Drifter is showing them all that she won't be at the tail end of the class! What she lacks in size she makes up for in heart and ability. She seems to enjoy jumping, and in 1966 she will be competing in more shows, in fact all the Quarter horse shows Johann can reach, as well as second-year green hunter classes.

Beginning this year at the Edmonton spring show, Johann and Drifter were entered in four events. They won the Quarter Horse jumping, the western pleasure, and placed in both the western riding and trail horse classes. Continuing her early 1966 wins, Drifter was entered in only one Quarter Horse event at the Calgary spring show in May. This was the western pleasure, which Johann said she won easily. This class was judged by Clyde Kennedy, who rode the mare himself, and was very pleased with her light mouth and her response to a rider.

Johann also entered her mare into the green lightweight hunter class at Calgary and placed fifth. She said Drifter looked like a pony with those fine, big Thoroughbreds.

At Red Deer later, this pair won third in the green hunter class, and then at Edmonton in May they won the green hunter class. And after three jump-offs in the intermediate jumping, they lost on time by three seconds.

Noches Drifter is quite a nervous and moody horse as well. Her disposition is good, and she is easy to handle. At times she will be quite lazy and other times she will be just the opposite. Jumping seems to quiet her for the pleasure and trail horse classes, wearing off some of that excess energy. Johann understands the mare's feelings and is able to cope easily with any of her mood changes.

When Lord Mountbatten came to Edmonton on Easter Sunday, he requested to see some of these Quarter Horses working different events to show just what this versatile breed can do. He had seen the cutting horses that were flown to England a few years ago, and they impressed him very much. So Johann and Noches Drifter were chosen to perform in jumping, and the mare gave a flawless performance.

In the capable hands of Cheryl Forst, both Drifter and Johann are progressing in fine style, and it is indeed a tribute to the Quarter horse to have such a competitor as Drifter giving top performance in so many events. In 1965 Drifter earned her Register of Merit in points received in cutting, western pleasure, western trail riding, trail horse, and jumping.

She will jump up to 4'6" very well, but Johann realizes the mistake some riders make of pushing their mounts too far before they are ready. So she is taking the mare slow and easy, and trying to keep that willingness in evidence. She realizes she has an outstanding horse, and she is going to see that Drifter remains just that.

The mare is quite timid around people, but she is a real pet to the Laskin family. She will come when called and likes to put her head on Johann's shoulder, close her eyes, and all enjoy the rubbing and petting she can get. She loads and hauls well and has never been any trouble to handle, even for Johann alone.

Added events for Drifter are the road hack class, and another popular class in Canadian shows, the adult and child class. Johann and Mark show together in this class, on Drifter and Mark's black pony that he calls Little Drifter. They have always placed well or won these classes.

Currently, the Laskins are looking forward to the time that Mark will be competing on Noches Drifter, not only in hunter classes but all youth classes.

Johann Laskin and the great black mare Noches Drifter will be very prominent in the shows of the future, to be sure. And we neglected to mention one of the most important contributors to the success of this pair… Johann's husband. No doubt this success of his horse-minded family is of great compensation.

MR. PRETTY BAR

September 1972

Everybody tries just a little bit harder when the golden horse, Mr. Pretty Bar, and his even prettier little rider, Julie Harrison, enter the arena. Because they have to! This pair is a threat in the timed events anywhere they go, even though Julie has been competing for just a short time, and only since early 1972, on Mr. Pretty Bar.

Always fond of horses, Julie had wanted to own one since she was a little girl. She had to wait until she was 13 before she got an unregistered mare named Velvet. The Harrison's lived in Great Falls, and the mare was kept at their cabin on Smith River, some distance from home, so Julie didn't get to ride nearly as much as she wanted.

But once there, she camped on Velvet all day, riding bareback all the time.

Julie says her next horse was an unregistered gelding by the great sire, Vegas Hardway. He was a greenbroke horse, and a handful for a small girl to work, and Julie said of him: "He threw me about ten times before I finally learned how to handle him, and keep his head up. He was really a challenge to me, and made me learn to ride in a hurry."

In the fall of 1968 she felt that she had mastered him, so she decided to enter a horse show the next spring in Great Falls. All winter she spent in practicing, and then after all the work and worry, the horse did not perform at all well, probably due to a different arena and other horses and people. Julie was very discouraged, but her mind was made up and she decided she needed a registered Quarter Horse for her next mount. Her father didn't quite see it that way, yet when they heard of a Vegas Hardway colt out of a mare bred by the Bird-tail Ranch at Simms, he bought the colt after a lot of discussions, even tears, and this was how Julie became the owner of Vegas Weather, or Lad as she called him. This was in the spring of 1969.

Julie said that, now that she owned this expensive new registered horse, her dad thought she should enter all the events possible. Her parents both enjoyed the barrel racing event especially, and so Julie started working Lad on the barrels. The woman who owned the place where Julie boarded her horse, was watching her work out one day, and mentioned it to Karen Mitchell, who owns Vegas Hardway. So Karen, a very accomplished horsewoman herself, coached Julie and did a great deal to encourage her to continue with her riding. Julie has this to say about Karen: "She's always had an encouraging word when I've needed it most, and she spent a lot of free time and effort on me and my horses."

Julie felt that Lad was the fastest horse she had ever seen, and it was apparent that she had a top barrel horse in the making. He was a smooth, easy-riding horse, and he loved to run, and many a time instead of going around the first barrel, he would take off around the arena. This was the first barrel horse Julie had trained, and it was no easy chore since she had no idea what was involved. But with Karen's help and a lot of work, Lad began to settle down and do the job right, and it was a very happy girl that tied for first place in the Novice Barrel Race at Ft. Benton in 1971. Julie felt that she had made the grade.

Karen, besides riding barrels and bending horses, cutting horses and both English and western pleasure, also was a jumping horse rider, and so Julie became interested in jumping also. She tried Lad, but he was just too excitable for a jumping horse, so Julie says, "Dad got out his checkbook again and we headed for the Winter Fair in Bozeman. I ended up buying a long, range 16 hand mare with Joe Reed and My Texas Dandy breeding. She turned out to be a pretty good jumping horse, ending up in the top 10 in the nation in Youth Jumping."

Then Julie's problems and heartaches began. The jumping horse, Greno Brandy, ran through a barbwire fence, cutting herself badly, so she was out of action for the rest of the season. And last fall, while rounding the first barrel in their home arena, Lad stepped wrong someway, shattering his right hind pastern bone. The Vet said there were no hopes for him, so the horse had to be put away.

Julie was heartbroken. After working so hard for success, and finally seeing some of it come her way, she lost one horse and had another one crippled, for how long she didn't know.

There was nothing to do but search for another horse. Julie just knew she would never find one to fit Lad's shoes, however the family put an ad in the Quarter Horse Journal, and after receiving calls and letters from all over the United States, she was almost bewildered as to the next move. The most attractive-sounding horses were so far away; some were too high-priced; others did not suit for one reason or another. In March she received a letter from July Bush in Nebraska, describing 3 barrel horses that she had for sale. Harrison's were especially interested in one of them, but when they called, the horse had already been sold. However a couple of days later, Judy called, saying she knew of a horse that was for sale, a little red run that was the fastest pole horse that she had ever seen, and he also was a good barrel horse. She said he made some mighty tough competition around there. This horse sounded so good to the Harrisons that they decided to drive to Nebraska and have a look.

Julie thought that Mr. Pretty Bar resembled Lad quite a lot, and that was one reason why she bought him. She said that Lad had a lot going for him, but Bar, as she calls Mr. Pretty Bar, has all that plus loads of personality. He is one of the horses that thinks he is human and really prefers people to horses, something of a Sugar Bars trait, and Julie tells a story about him reaching his head over the stall door at the Helena Quarter Horse Show, and taking a big bite out of her sister's bologna sandwich! He really seemed to enjoy it too.

Mr. Pretty Bar was sired by Bar Fleet by Sugar Bars. The dam of Bar Fleet was Poco Rose by Poco Bay by Poco Bueno. Poco Bay is an AQHA Champion. His dam was Dolly D by Blackburn.

The dam of Mr. Pretty Bar was Pretty Mite, a dun mare that was by Corky Waggoner, and out of Under Heaven. Corky Waggoner's sire was He Mite by Garcia Silvertone, and his dam was Waggoner 11 by Blackburn. Under Heaven was sired by Underwood Chief by Golden Chief, and out of a Bell Ranch mare.

Lila Launer had trained Mr. Pretty Bar for barrel racing and pole bending. She followed 5 or 6 previous owners, who tried to make a pleasure horse of Bar, but he preferred the speed events, and though he is far from a flighty or excitable horse, he is always on his toes and ready to run. Julie works with him in youth Barrels and Poles, and turns right around and enters the All-Age classes as well. Her first barrel race horse, however, was in the college rodeo at Montana Start University in April. She came out 4th in a field of about 40 contestants, and she was real pleased for their first try. She plans to try for the rodeo team with him next year.

At the All Youth Stampede in Great Falls in 1972, Julie and Bar won the barrel race. She went to the Billings Saddle Club Show later, and won a second in barrel racing.

At the Choteau rodeo, she placed 4th in barrel racing, and in the big Missoula Quarter Horse Show, they came away with the trophy for first in the all-ages barrel race.

At the Kalispell Quarter Horse show, Julie and Bar won second in youth barrels, 3rd in youth poles, and 4th in all-ages barrel racing.

At Ft. Benton, they won the youth poles and barrels, and the all-ages pole bending. A few days later Julie talked herself into entering the rodeo at Ft. Benton, and she and Bar tied for first place.

A foot injury caused Bar to be laid up for a time during the show season, but he recovered completely, and the pretty pair made a most impressive showing their first few months in competition. Next year will tell a different story, with Julie more used to contesting, and she and Mr. Pretty Bar will make their competition hurry quite a lot more! It is great to ride good horses that can win for you, and greater yet to ride a winning horse that is as handsome as is Mr. Pretty Bar. Julie can well be proud of the golden horse, and the Harrisons can be mighty proud of their lovely daughter as she rides into the arena, for this is just a pair that really catches the eye wherever they go. And they have proved that "pretty is as pretty does."

BARREL RACING ARIST ELSA JENSEN

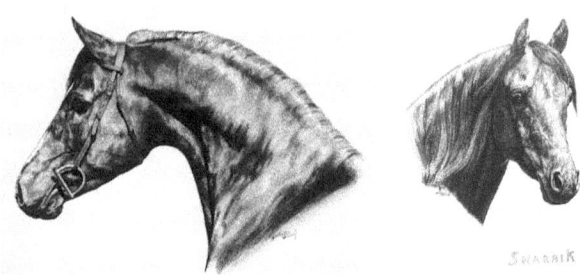

A new star in the Arabian Art World has risen in the form of Elsa Jensen, barrel racer from Moses Lake, Washington. This is a new line for Elsa, who has been a Quarter Horse fancier for several years. She has turned out some beautiful portraits of Quarter Horses, and many of the best breeders are proud of a "Jensen portrait." Her drawings of rodeo scenes are full of action and interest also, and she has some portraits of Thoroughbreds to show as well.

Elsa was born in Detroit, and came to Washington when she was just 4 years old. She has ridden and handled horses since she was just a little girl, and is a very accomplished horsewoman. Much of her time is spent in training their Quarter horses, and up until the past year when work demanded so much of her time, she was off to the rodeos every weekend to barrel race. In 1961 she and her faithful little bay mare Lenna, won the Washington State Championship, and the beautiful trophy saddle. Lenna was a very consistent barrel horse, and from the time Elsa started working her on the barrels in 1958, until the fall of 1962, they failed to place but five times, and each time by knocking a barrel over.

Elsa is married to rancher-calf roper Jerry Jensen, a former Idaho boy, and they are ranching near Moses Lake. Besides Quarter Horses, they are starting in the Angus cattle business at this time. In their early twenties, this young couple seems to have a very bright future.

While on a visit to Hot Springs, Montana, with Bill and Fay Haynes, Elsa became interested in portraying Arabian horses. Through their mutual interest in Quarter Horses, the Haynes and Jensens became acquainted, and since Bill and Fay also run some grade Arabian mares and a registered stallion, they naturally favor Arabs along with the Quarter horses. Elsa's first work of Jule Bar (Sugar Bars-Juleo) and Fay in a barrel racing and pole bending pose, hangs on the wall in the Haynes home, and astounds everyone with its perfection and naturalness.

At first Elsa was reluctant to try drawing Arabians, being unfamiliar with this breed of horses, but with some encouraging, she decided to give it a try. She took home some copies of the *Arabian Horse News*, and some time later turned out beautiful portraits of Mujahid, owned by Mr. and Mrs. Richard Newman, Golden Colorado; Ferneyn, owned by Harvey Ellis, Chatsworth, California; and Natez and Serafix, owned by John H. Rogers, Walnut Creek, California. These drawings came with apologies for ""not doing better," but they are beautifully done and a credit to any artist. They defy improvement, and one cannot fail to recognize the horses in the pictures. However, like many artists, Elsa is never satisfied with her work.

She refuses to "touch up" or exaggerate a picture or change a horse's looks in any way. Her portraits must be as much like the live horse as possible, and she has that rare ability to portray each horse exactly as it is. She captures the life and personality of the horses, and each one is an individual in itself, and not just a stiff copy with the color changed, as is the case so many times.

She works from photographs, and there is no chance that the finished product will ever be mistaken for any other horse. Else is taking orders now for Arabian portraits, and she is interested in making this new venture a success along with her other work.

Arabian enthusiasts love to see their favorite horses in art, and this little Washington barrel racer artist can copy them to perfection! It is with pride that we welcome her to our Arabian Art World.

THEY ARE ALL TOP HANDS!

Good riders on top horses have always been a winning combination, and when you look at the 6 Ogilvie's from Florence, Montana, you are looking at 6 potential champions. This family, from parents Ethel and Alex down to little Rinda, are horse people through and through. They have all known horses from the time they were tiny, horses of all kinds, sizes, and breeds, and today they are all mounted on registered Quarter horses.

Alex was born October 1, 1924, at Cohagen, Montana, back in the wild horse and cattle country. He learned the hard way how to handle horses of every kind, and he had some good teachers. But a lot of his knowledge came first hand through his own experiences. Right now it would take a book to record even part of his experiences with horses, wild ones, tame ones, and all those in-between kinds. Alex knows them all and he knows them well.

Part of his earlier life was spent in Colorado, and surprisingly enough, at one time he taught school in the Missouri River breaks of eastern Montana. He didn't have a car, but he had good saddlehorses, and appeared on one for his first day of school. He figured that was a better mode of transportation anyhow, and less expensive!

The day before he started his school-teaching career, he had won a beautiful big trophy at the Jordan Labor Day rodeo, and in the saddle bronc riding event. Alex Contested at several Amateur rodeos, and he loved it. He didn't like his school teaching job, so he didn't remain with that for long. He worked for Bud Kramer, Cohagen, off and on for 5 years, breaking horses. And when a cowboy rode for Kramer, he rode! They had hundreds of horses, most of them running wild, and it took a bronc rider to ride most of them when they were fresh off the range.

In those days, saddle horses were one of the main methods of travel in that country, and Alex was known to ride in to Jordan 30 miles when the roads were snowed in, to see his girlfriend (later his wife) who attended high school there. It wasn't too far into town, but oh, that long ride home!

Alex doesn't do any saddle bronc or bareback riding at rodeos anymore. He contests in team roping however, and picks up now and then in the riding events. But not long ago he thrilled the crowd at a Missoula County Fair, in the wild horse race. He had a big black bronc, quite a bucking horse, and he sat up straight, spurred and quirted that horse in the fashion of the old-time cowboys. The crowd went wild, for they were viewing a part of the old west in modern days. The fellows like to have Alex for a pardner in the wild horse race because he understands "earing" and handling those wild horses with ease.

Ethel Ogilvie was born May 11, 1932, at Olympia, Washington, and was raised in Eastern Montana between Calf Creek and the Missouri River. Her parents, Hartley and Della Lambert, were raised on the Lower Musselshell River. They had horses and cattle on a ranch of 60 sections of deeded and leased land at Sand Springs. Hartley broke a lot of horses, and often while he went to eat dinner he would leave a horse saddled in the corral, or as he said, "put one on to cook." Now and then they would miss Ethel, and going to the corral they would find her approaching a horse, trying to talk to it in Hartley's language and tone of voice, and saying "Come here!" while yanking on the rope. Once they caught her trying to mount one of the broncs, a horse Hartley had only ridden once. They were afraid Ethel would get hurt, but Della says, "somehow horses seem to know, and from the time she was a baby, Ethel had a great love for horses and dogs. And they seemed to try anything to please her."

Ethel and her mother used to ride a lot together. One morning real early in the spring, Della was riding her saddle horse for the first time since the fall before. He had been running on the range and was feeling real good. They started out on a jog trot, and as they hit a little downward slope and broke into a lope, Della's horse bogged his head and bucked her off. It happened so fast she had no chance to stop him, or to stay on. Ethel was just a little girl at the time, and she was real mad at her mother's horse. She caught him, got on, and gave him a good spurring.

In 1950, the Lamberts moved to Stevensville, where they still live. They raise Quarter Horses and Thoroughbreds, and do some showing and racing. When they can get away, they go to Tucson for the winter, where they own 5 acres with a nice duplex home, and 12 box stalls for their horses. This stands right across from Rillito race track. Then when spring comes, they return to Montana and spend their summers at horse shows, Fairs, and races. Poco Cisco, beautiful buckskin grandson of Poco Dell, and Flying Twister by Okie Twister, a many-times champion mare, are but two of their well-known string of show horses.

When Ethel was 4, her dad gave her a yearling black and white pinto colt, her very first horse. His name was Paint, and as soon as the colt was big enough to ride, Hartley would saddle him up, and Paint and Ethel would be off. She tells this of one of her trips: "Once when I was a few miles from home, the saddle turned and I couldn't get it uncinched, so I held him over to a stump, climbed on and rode him home with the saddle dangling under his belly. I had a terrier dog that rode behind the saddle most of the time too."

Alex and Ethel met at a rodeo in 1946. They were both entered in the 1/2-mile saddle horse race, and Ethel says, "Guess the one thing that impressed me most was Alex beat me and won the race."

Alex hadn't been back too long from World War II at that time. He was in the Marines from 1942 to 1945, with Paratroopers. He spent time in the Solomon Islands, Iwo Jima, and was wounded at Bouganville.

It was in 1949 that Alex and Ethel started going together steady, and then on June 17, 1951, they were married at Stevensville.

For a while, they lived on their folks' ranch at Sand Springs, and from there they used to go to rodeos and O-Mok-Sees. This was the start of Ethel's barrel racing. She loved the competition and excitement, and she was always in there trying to win. She and Alex won 9 trophies at the Glasgow State O-Mok-See one year. He was high point man, and she was high point woman at that show.

Ethel's first barrel horse was Buttons, a little dark chestnut gelding that was 1/2 Arabian and 1/2 Quarter Horse. He had stockings and a blaze face, a beautiful little horse that weighed only about 850 pounds. Ethel was fond of Buttons, and this team set out to show the girls how to barrel race. By this time barrel racing was in Ethel's blood "like betting on the races," and she didn't miss any of them if she could help it. Buttons was an honest, dependable little horse, and it was a proud moment when Ethel and Buttons won the barrel race at the Roy rodeo, and their first buckle! This was about 1952. From then on they won quite a bit of money, more buckles and trophies, and a lot of publicity. In 1959, Ethel sold Buttons to Viola Thomas of Calgary, and the next year Viola won the championship saddle with him. It was a sad day however when Buttons left, because by that time the little Ogilvie girls were riding him too. There were 3 of them by that time, Marty, Della, and Alex. Rinda came along last, and she is now 5 years old.

While Alex and Ethel were on the ranch at Sand Springs, her mother would write from Stevensville and tell them of any rodeo west of the mountains, and they would load up and head west for the Bitterroot country. They like the climate and decided they'd like to live there, so they bought at 500 acre place about 1/2 mile from the river. In the summer the girls get their inner tubes and their horses, and head for the river where they spend any happy hours. The horses soak their feet in the water and roll in the sand while the girls play in the water and swim.

Ogilvie's started a registered Quarter Horse gelding they called Copper, by Pride out of Miss Peaches, to replace Buttons. He became a good barrel horse that carried Ethel to a number of wins. Gradually the two older girls took him over however, and Ethel started contesting on Blackie, or Bushmel, a registered Quarter Horse stallion of Chubby breeding, that turned into one of the best barrel horses in the Northwest country. A small, compact little horse, Blackie could run pretty well, but he made up for the fact that he wasn't a racehorse by not wasting a single jump during his runs. He was the talk of the country for several years for his barrel racing ability.

1962 was Blackie's first season of steady use. He had cut a hind leg severely in February of that year, and for a while it looked as though he wouldn't never run. But in May that year Ethel and Blackie won the Diamond Spur barrel race at Spokane, which was a GRA contract at the Spokane Quarter Horse show that spring.

In July 1962, High River, Alberta held its first All-Girl rodeo, and they had a purse of a thousand dollars up in the barrel race. Of course Ethel was on hand, and came back home the winner to the tune of $646. By the end of the year, her total winnings amounted to over $2300, which put Ethel in the number 2 spot in the Montana Barrel Racers Association standings for the year. Blackie earned his Register of Merit rating in barrel racing that year also.

1963 saw Blackie win the award for Montana's high-point barrel horse in AQHA competition. And more than that, he carried Ethel to the MBRA Championship for the year, and they were presented a beautiful trophy saddle which was made by DeVore's of Helena. This was a great honor, and Ethel said "I give all the credit to Blackie for his honesty and consistency, and his will to run under any conditions. It's good to look back and think of some of his good runs."

Ethel team-ropes with Alex in their arena at home, and she does a little calf roping and goat tying also. Unintentionally a couple of years ago she entertained the huge crowd in the Stampede Corral in Calgary, where she was entered in the barrel race and goat tying. She drew the first run on a great big, tough-acting white goat that must have had it in for pretty cowgirls. She rode to him, dismounted and was after him in fine style, but the goat refused to cooperate and gave Ethel a few hard kicks. She got it down, and those 4 feet went to wind-milling, and the goat kept struggling, but determined Ethel stayed with it until she got it tied. Her snowy-white ruffled shirt was goat tracks from shoulder to waist, and she even had hoof prints on her face. As she rode out of the arena, she was mad. Usually even-tempered and good-natured, she said, "If there hadn't been so many people in there I'd have stomped that thing in the ground!"

Ogilvie's see to it that their children are always well-mounted. They ride good horses and they know good horses, and they see to it that there is always a saddle empty and waiting, "ever since the kids were born." Luckily they are all crazy about horses, and they spend most of their free time with them.

Ethel tells about winning a Shetland pony at a Fair in Jordan for $1.00, and he used to pick little Marty (the oldest girl) up by the tail of her coat. He bucked the girls off more times than they rode him, so soon he was sold, and replaced with a Quarter Horse mare. If they got spilled off they'd get right back on. They never gave up and they weren't easy to scare. Hartley always told Ethel that was the way you were supposed to. Never give up. She got bucked off 3 times one day, and he kept saying, "Get up and get back on," so she did. And she raised her girls the same way. They all work hard and train hard, keeping their horses in shape and ready to work.

Alex deals a lot in horses, so the girls have had experience with every kind, not just the gentle ones. Marty and Della can, and do, ride a lot of horses some pretty good hands would pass up. They have had some bad times all right, but luckily nothing too serious.

Once Marty was riding a little bay horse called Peter Pan, bareback, with a binder twine around his neck. They were playing Cowboys and Indians at the time. Alexa was on her little POA pony, Cookie, all dressed up in war paint and feathers, and when Marty rode around the corner of the house, the sight was too much for Peter Pan, he threw Marty on the cement step, puncturing an intestine. She went to the hospital, and Ethel said, "Two weeks and $900 later, she was back home rearin' to ride again."

Alexa was riding once when she was 4 years of age, when a loose horse spooked her mount and it ran away. Tiny, blonde Alexa was barefooted, clinging to the horse, pulling for all she was worth and yelling, "Help!" The horse ran about a mile, jumped 3 big ditches, and headed home on high, picking up speed all the way. He came to a halt at the corral gate and Alexa kept going. She hit her head on a corral pole, shed a few tears as she sat up and said, "Boy mama, I was really goin' fast!"

Della got on a new horse one day and headed for the river. She got to a ditch and the horse decided not to go and started to buck. Della had overshoes on, and she got one hooked on the saddle horn somehow, and was hanging with her head down while the horse bucked in a circle. Luckily, Alex was near and ran out and stopped the horse before Della was injured.

Little Rinda has had her ups and downs also. She has her own horse, a little bay called Doodle-bug. He is a 4 year old, by the great horse Whirlie by Tamo. When Rinda and Alex were out riding one day, a windstorm came up and blew a cardboard box up close to Doodle-bug. He ran off and Alex had to act as pickup man and catch her. Another time one of the sheepdogs jumped a gate, spooked the horse and he took off and left Rinda behind. But she still wouldn't trade him for anything.

At the Stevensville Horse Show in 1966, she won a trophy and a blue ribbon, her first wins, and she was one proud little girl! Everyone else in her family had been winning, and now she was "one of them." She also barrel raced at the Hamilton Fair. When they called her name, she came running from outside the arena, and when the flagger dropped the flag, Doodle-bud stopped dead still. With some persuasion, they continued their run. She ran all 3 days of the Fair, and the only thing she couldn't understand was "Why didn't I get some money?"

When Marty, the pretty, slender blonde with the twinkle in her eyes, was 3, Ethel was exercising her barrel horse at a Roundup rodeo. She got through and let Marty lead him, only to come back and find a girl riding the horse, and Marty playing with a big balloon. Marty had traded the horse for the balloon, and she thought at the time it was a pretty good trade. Both Marty and Della learned to barrel race on Copper. He was gentle and dependable, and made good runs for them. Once at a barrel race in Ronan, they both used him, and tied for first place. When Ethel started a new bay gelding, Ponder's Pride, Marty fell heir to Blackie. They hit it off well together, and Blackie seemed to like this little lightweight rider.

Marty's first year contesting on Blackie earned her third place in the MBRA standings, with nearly a thousand dollars won. One of her best wins was at Rapid City, South Dakota, where she won the 2-run average against some top contestants, many of them GRA members. It was pretty stiff competition, but the combination of Marty and Blackie could match it. Marty has won many buckles, trophies, and ribbons since then.

Della, second to Marty, started riding Copper when she was only 6. She tied for first at a horse show in the Field house in Missoula against 17 barrel racers, and won her first trophy that year. A beautiful girl with long, auburn hair, she now rides a big Palomino gelding, Palobar by Leo Bar, and out of a Plaudit mare. Palobar is one-eyed, nevertheless he is a top barrel horse. He can run like a race-horse and when he work the barrels right, he is a difficult horse to beat. Della had her troubles with him earlier, when she first started him. She was just a slip of a girl, and this big horse at full speed was too much for her at times. Her first rodeo on him, the KO near Missoula, created some excitement when he ran away with her and almost ran over the photographer. Then the next day, Ethel, Marty and Della loaded up and went to the Cascade rodeo, where Della and Palobar won second place. She has won several buckles, and was the MBRA Rookie of the Year in 1965, winning a beautiful trophy.

Ponder's Pride, Ethel's new bay horse, was the Lambert's good horse Ponder by Red Concho by Red Dog. Lambert's gave the horse to Ethel for her birthday. His dam, Second Gear, by Kingwood, was a mare they prized highly. Ponder's Pride's first season barrel racing won 5th place in the MBRA standings for his mistress.

Then they got into the habit of tipping barrels, and this was one habit neither Alex nor Ethel could correct. So she started a full sister of his, a pretty sorrel filly called Ponder's Lady. This mare carried Ethel to 5th in the MBRA standings in 1966, her first year of contesting. She suffered a serious quarter crack, and went lame. This has laid her up for almost a year, but Ethel has hopes of continuing on Ponder's Lady this coming rodeo season.

Usually Ethel and the girls travel together. They have a nice big camper on their pickup, and pull a 4-horse trailer, and they spend a lot of time on the road. It is a lot of fun, but Ethel says, "There is no place like home." They have had good and bad times while traveling, but nothing very serious; a few flat tires, and once the canvas top blew off the trailer in a windstorm. But Ethel says, "We've had a lot of fun in spite of our troubles, split seams and busted zippers."

Tragedy struck the Ogilvies on January 4, 1964. They had left home for a short time, and while they were gone the house burned to the ground. They lost everything; clothes, furniture, treasures, and keepsakes that could never be replaced; trophies, ribbons, belt buckles, pictures... they lost 25 trophies, 130 ribbons, and 12 belt buckles. No one had a belt on that day, so not even a buckle was saved.

Later while digging through the ashes and debris, Ethel found all that was left of her beautiful trophy saddle, the saddle which she won as the MBRA State Champion in 1963... the metal from the stirrups. She stood there holding one of the stirrups, tears streaming down her face. It was then that friends came to her rescue, and when DeVores agreed to make a duplicate saddle at cost, they chipped in and paid for the new one. This saddle is Ethel's most prized trophy, partly because she won the State Championship, and partly because it is a remembrance of her many friends and their thoughtfulness.

You can't quit in the face of misfortune, and Ogilvies soon went to work and built a new home, a log house that is a show place, a beautiful ranch home.

There will be 4 registered Quarter Horses in the long 4-horse trailer this year, with Ethel, Marty, Della, and Alexa all competing, and soon little Rinda will probably join them as a contestant. Much of the time now she goes with her daddy on his horse-trading and rodeo or horse-show trips.

When you see the 4 of them unloading, cleaning and exercising their horses, and contesting, you may think you are looking at 4 sisters rather than a mother and 3 daughters. Youthful, slender and with a vibrant personality, Ethel can pass for an older sister. But a proud mother she is, and seeing to it that her daughters will carry on as top contestants with the ability and sportsmanship that made her so popular to friends and rodeo fans. Sharing their love of horses, sports, and competition, the Ogilvies will be on the road and in the news for a long time to come.

MONTANA BARREL RACE WINNERS (CREDIT APPALOOSA NEWS - MAY 1967)

The Montana Barrel Racers are known for their top horses and their ability to ride and win. Each year the MBRA holds a Championship Finals, which includes a Novice Barrel Race for girls and horses having won less than $100 in MBRA competition. Some of these novice contestants are riding horses they are starting to replace the old faithful barrel horse; others are girls or women who have barrel raced for years, but not with the association; and still others are newcomers anxious to join the ranks of rodeo and horse show contestants in barrel racing.

Whoever they are, generally they are mounted on the very best in horse flesh, and each year the competition is keener.

The 1966 MBRA Finals were held at Sidney in Eastern Montana, in conjunction with the Fair and Rodeo. The Novice Barrel Race was being run off, with a first class group of barrel racers bringing the crowd to its feet with each run. Contestants were riding like professionals, and horses performing the same.

But the one who thrilled the most was Linda Lightfield of Lambert, Montana and her Appaloosa gelding, Dusty. Linda and Dusty made a flawless run to win the beautiful BRA trophy which is awarded annually to the Novice Champion of the year.

A sophomore in high school, Linda is 15 years old, and has been competing in rodeo and horse shows for 9 years. She has won many trophies, belt buckles, and ribbons, including two high-point trophies for the Northeastern Division of Montana Saddle Clubs in 1963 and 1964. She won the Northeastern Division Saddle Club

Barrel Race Championship in the 12-16 year age group in '63, '64, and '66.

Linda raised her Appaloosa horse, Dusty, but sold him to a neighbor as a yearling. By the time he was three, Dusty was her toughest competition in Saddle Club and rodeo events, which is quite an accomplishment for a horse so young. He won many trophies for his owner during his first year in competition.

Last spring, Linda's barrel horse fell with her at the High School Rodeo in Miles City and was crippled, so their neighbor decided to sell Dusty back to her.

Dusty immediately came down with a sever case of distemper, however, he recovered in time to help Linda win the Northeastern Division Saddle Club barrel race, and the MBRA Novice barrel race at Sidney. She had only been able to ride him twice before going to Sidney, but the little horse is very anxious to please, and gives his best at every run.

Dusty is six, and was sired by Shiek's Danny T-1260, owned by Mae Hartsook of Chester, Montana, a well-known breeder of quality Appaloosas. His dam was a grade mare.

Bringing a lot of color and action to the barrel racing sport, Linda and the horse Dusty will be seen again this year, adding more trophies to their collecting and giving a lot of publicity to the Appaloosa breed.

Linda Lightfield and Dusty

Montana Barrel Race Winner

BILLY KEENE

Billy Keene was a Trick Rider, Bull Fighter, and Rodeo Clown. He would stay at the Poloson Ranch whenever he was working a rodeo in Western Montana.

Billy worked rodeos all over the western and southern states. His trained Trick Horse, Tony, was retired on the Poloson Ranch in 1955.

Fay and Billy Keen

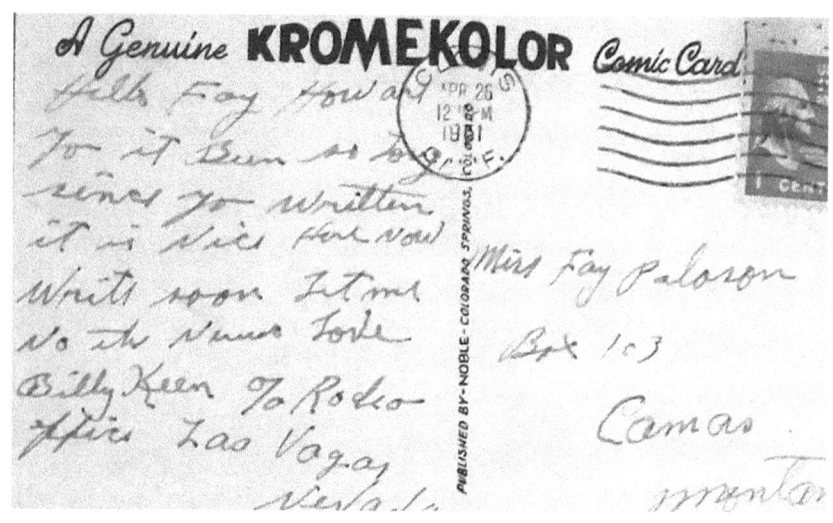

Card from Billy when he was rodeoing in Nevada. 1 of many cards sent to Fay & the Poloson Family. The cards are in the LaRue Hot Springs Museum.

JOHN HERMAN

Up in the North end of the Little Bitterroot Valley in northwestern Montana is what is called the Big Draw and Hog Heaven country. The Big Draw runs from east to west, and the highway now runs along this valley from Elmo to Niarada. Running north and south is Hog Heaven, a big flat which allegedly got its name from an epidemic which took the lives of great number of hogs there at one time.

Joe Herman figured prominently in the early history of the Flathead, as this country is commonly called. A giant of a man both in statue and holdings, John had a lot of grit in the days when that was a very desirable trait. Times were none too easy in the early days of ranching in Montana. The people endured many hardships, but not being too used to much luxury, they made the best of it and got along, and they enjoyed life. Neighbored helped each other without asking for pay except help in return when it was needed. (Surprisingly enough, this practice still goes on in most of the real ranching areas.)

Joe Herman was born in 1866 in Virginia City, Montana, where his father, Jacob, had a blacksmith shop. Jacob was a son of the Old Country, migrated to Pennsylvania from Germany. Later he came to the mining town of Butte, Montana, and then went to Virginia City in the gold rush days. His wife, known later as Grandmother Herman, came from Pennsylvania with her family in a covered wagon. Her father was a section foreman at Plains, Montana, when the railroad was built. Horse Plains it was called then, because it was a wide-open country that afforded wonderful grazing for wild horses in the early days.

From Virginia City, the Jacob Herman family moved to Thompson Falls. There were four boys, Mike, Chris, George and John. Jacob homesteaded on what is now the site of the Thomson Falls Dam, and eventually sold the land to the Montana Power Company. He was paid off in cash, in thousand-dollar bills. He fell in with the wrong companions, and was robbed of all the money, and was unable to recover any of it.

Jacob had a freight route from Thompson Falls to Kellogg and Wallace, Idaho, in those days. These towns were prosperous mining towns then, and John, though still quite young, drove freight teams over this rough, torturous route. Even then John was a good businessman, and he bought a piece of land, 160 acres in size, at the mouth of the canyon through which the road passed. Travelers going over the pass either went through his land and paid a toll charge, or attempted going around over almost impossible terrain. John made some enemies here, but to him it was business. He was out to make himself some money. He had some trouble with travelers, who tried to force their way, but John was tough and he was big, and he didn't bluff easy. If he couldn't back up his stand with his bare fists, he could use a gun, and soon word got around that John Herman was a tough character, so they paid the toll and traveled his route.

John hauled passengers over this roadless route also, and had to tie some of them in coaches to keep them from falling out! It was that rough. Quite a skinner at an early age, John also drove a bull train, hauling freight from Drummond to Helena. He was at that time in his teens.

At one time John had a pack outfit of about eighty head of horses and mules, and he freighted from Fisher River country West of Kalispell to Missoula. He took supplies and equipment from Missoula to Fisher River for the miners and their mines, and on his return trip, he packed deer meat for Missoula business places. His trip took him through Pleasant Valley, through the Bitterroot, and on to Missoula.

Eventually John Herman met a girl from California who was living at Eddy, near Thompson Falls. Her name was Vergie Anderson. When they decided to get married, he rode horseback from Thompson Falls to Missoula, which was the county seat, to get the license. It was about 200 miles round trip, and he had to ford the river going and coming. They were married in 1895 at Thompson Falls.

Vergie and John had two sons, John Otho (Coke) and L.G. Coke was born March 7, 1897 at Kalispell, and L.G. was born February

25, 1899, also at Kalispell. John was proud of his little family, and he loved them deeply, though he wasn't one to demonstrate his affections.

He couldn't tolerate cheats or liars, and his word was his bond. He was slow to anger, and had the happiest, most carefree personality. But he wasn't a man you could push too far! He had a reputation for fair and honest dealings, and he had a lot of friends. He was a shrewd dealer and businessman, and at one time his holdings were tremendous. He was a good cowboy and an exceptional cowman; he knew cattle. And he could ride a horse well, though unlike many of the early-day young men of the west, he was not a bronc rider.

In the early 1900's the Herman family got the urge to change their location, so they left Thompson Falls. George and Coke got themselves a mine over in the Ferry Basin country northeast of Perma, which didn't prove too prosperous. John and Vergie bought some land in Hog Heaven, coming there on horseback. They were there several years before the country was opened to homesteading, and had made themselves a pretty good stake by that time, and had built their cow herd up considerably. They owned enough land for a foothold, and ran their cattle mainly on the Indian reservation, as did most of the ranchers of that day. This wasn't really approved of by the higher-ups, but if a man knew the right people and treated them well, nothing was said

Hay was scarce in that country and was valuable property then. They didn't use it unless they had to. Herman's raised some hay on their home place, and bought straw stacks up around Kalispell, and a little wild hay in the Marion and Brown's Meadow area. This hay didn't amount to much. It was mainly slough hay which was mostly "stuffing." The hay, of course, was hauled by teams and wagons, or sleds, and it was a long, hard job. All the work that is done by machine now, was performed by horsepower then, and they used a lot of horses. And they used a lot of men too.

They raised their own work horses on the ranch, as well as saddle stock. At one time they owned between three and four hundred head. Herman's horses were mainly Standardbred and Hambletonian, find, big horses, mostly bay in color, with stamina and cow sense. They were usually not broken to ride until they were used hard. And they generally needed a lot of work to get them gentled down. Those horses made cowboys out of a lot of young fellows! Coke especially, was a salty bronc rider in his day.

Horses weren't worth much then, since there were so many of them everywhere. In the 1930's, Hermans sold over 200 head of range horses to be used for fox feed, for $5 a head.

Cattle and horses had the run of the country then, from up north of Hog Heaven to Elmo by Flathead lake, on south down the Little Bitterroot to the Big Bend country where a lot of stock wintered, due to the good grass and mild winters. This entire area was noted for mild winters for that matter, and with no fences to hold cattle; they drifted with the storms and found grass to tide them through the winter if their owners could not get to them. They were better off scattered to the four winds where they could locate their own grass when it was unusually bad, than to be confined in a small place with scarcely enough hay or straw to keep them alive. Death losses were sometimes heavy, but running expenses were small, so they figured they could afford the loss rather than put a lot of money in hard-to-get feed. Spring was always welcome to both stockmen and livestock in those days, as it is today.

When the country was homesteaded, that put a stop to a lot of the cowboy's easy way of life. In 1910, land outside the Indian reservation was opened by Congress to homesteading. Tracts were set aside for Indian allotments, power sites, and school districts. Then people had to register at the Land Office and draw numbers for their new land. As writer John Rhone of Hot Springs said, "There was an optimist for every 160." And optimists they were, for a while at least.

Small stores, post offices, and schools sprang up. Niarada post office was begun by Gene Riley in 1911. It is still in operation, by Mr. and Mrs. Bill Wood. Eudora post office and store was started in 1911 by a Mr. Troutman. It was later sold to Mr. Yates, and eventually was closed. Now all that remains of Eudora is a pile of rocks and some old rotted logs and poles. Of the schools, Lower Battle Butte is still operating. Most of the land was taken soon, but few of the settlers were familiar with the country. Not many of them lasted much longer than it took to prove up on the homestead. John Herman bought much of this land for next to nothing.

Cattle ranching was John's life, and his ranching venture expanded until he owned over 7000 acres, and some State leases. The "Round-top T" brand was in evidence for miles in every direction on both horses and cattle.

John and Vergie beloved strongly in education, and they had a tutor at the ranch for their sons, a lovely lady from back east, Mrs. Poe, who with her husband made an attempt at homesteading and had failed. Later the boys attended high school at Kalispell, and for two years Coke went to the University of Pennsylvania. L.G. was a self-made veterinarian, a practice which came in handy to many of the ranchers and farmers in later years.

John Herman took pride in his home, and the big log house and outbuildings, made of logs by master ax-men, hand-hewn and carefully put together, still stand today as a cow camp for the Ed Conrad Ranch. The logs in the house were dove-tailed at the corners, and the Herman yard was a show place with a neat picket fence and its of shrubs and flowers. They planted an orchard which is still producing. Water has no problem, as they had a fine spring near the buildings. They burned wood of course, in those days. Wood logs were snaked by a team down from the nearby hills, sawed by hand into blocks, then split with an ax and wedge into whatever size was needed for heaters and cook stoves. A fine, lively, warm heat that nothing in these modern days can replace! There was nothing however, that could do away with the ashes and soot and "stove black." But at that time no one complained too much, because that was the only way to heat and cook. Electricity didn't come to that part of the country until 1952.

There was a lot of open country when the Hermans started in the cow business, but homesteading, other ranchers, and fences, took a lot out of the once-free range, and over-grazing took its toll eventually. So they trailed their cattle all over the country to pasture. Potomac and Helmville, up the Blackfoot River, and later to the Big Hole Basin near Wisdom. This last move was made in 1919, and was a turning point in the lives of the Herman family. With an especially dry year, overgrazing, and a scarcity of hay in the Flathead, John Herman decided to try and locate a place where he could put up some hay as well as have more pasture. So in 1919 he went to the famed Big Hole Basin and dealt for the Spokane Ranch and its cattle. Mainly he wanted all that hay the Basin was noted for. He shipped his cattle to the Divide Railroad Station, and trailed into the Big Hole from there.

He got together a crew to put up hay on his new ranch, and they went to work. At one time they had 120 men on the job, and they butchered a beef every other day to feed them. In those days if a man wanted a job and would work, he didn't have to go far. It was no 8-hour shift with coffee breaks and big benefits either. It was until you got the job done, often from before daylight until long past dark. A man did an honest day's work for his pay, and a good boss appreciated it. So did the hired man if he had a speck of pride and honesty. Their haying was done with horses, of course, and they used a lot of work teams.

When cowmen gather, it is a cinch one of the main topics of conversation will be the weather. If it's a fair winter day they feel lucky and maybe they will reminisce about the bad winter last year, how the snow piled up, and so on. From there the talk may lead to some severe blizzards of the past, usually many years ago. Maybe one old timer will say: "Storms ain't as tough as they usta be." Maybe they aren't, and maybe it's simply because times have changed and things are easier and handier now so the in climate weather may be more easily coped with.

After the winter of 1919-1920, John Herman was in a first-rate position to tell about the ravages of winter. He was in the Big Hole at this time. That was a bad winter. It came early in the fall with 2 feet of snow and 20 below zero weather, and it stayed that way. Herman's fed up all their hay. Then, to make matters worse, the bank foreclosed on Herman and took his cattle in the early spring. The fall before, the cattle prices had been high and hay was almost worth its weight in gold, but then toward spring, the bottom dropped out of the cattle market, and hay continued to rise. (Even potatoes sold for $20 a sac!) With the deep snow there wasn't a chance for cattle to graze.

According to Frank McDowell, "Herman was taking a long shot and he missed. It was just one of those things." Frank and his sons Mel, Bob and Sam, now own the old Spokane Ranch, along with other vast holdings in the Big Hole Basin.

Winter that year lasted until the middle of May. Jack Anderson, an old-timer in that country, and father-in-law of Sam McDowell, helped drive the Herman cattle in from Tye Creek with a part Indian fellow, Joe Brooks, who worked for Herman, and John's son, L.G.

Jack was riding for Carl Huntley at that time, and he said he can still remember how that, being young and full of hell, they drove the cattle into a deep hole in the river and swam them around awhile before moving them out, and they fashioned break-aways in their lariats with wire, to practice roping all the way in to the Spokane Ranch.

Jack Anderson helped drive the cattle from ranch to ranch, feeding up hay owned by ranchers who owed the Wisdom Bank. This was the bank's way of collecting its interest.

The snow was so deep when they left the Elliott Ranch, they had to break a trail with saddlehorses. The snow was as high as the calf's back, a good 3 1/2 feet. They got a good cow dog from one rancher, or they'd never have moved the cattle to the next feedground. After the hay was gone and still no break in the weather, Carl Huntley sold some steers and fed the Herman cattle for the bank, with hay at $60 a ton.

Anderson said, "Herman wasn't the only one to go broke that winter. It was truly a winter to remember."

Herman's had a few head of cattle that the boys and Joe Brooks had held out for wages, a Standardbred stallion that cost $1500 (but was mortgaged,) their saddlehorses, and a 30.30 rifle. They headed for the Flathead country on horseback, and it must have been a sorry outfit. On the way home the Standardbred stallion died, to top off their troubles!

But John Herman wasn't a quitter, and he wasn't one to cry over failures. He didn't feel too sorry for himself; his terrible failure merely slowed him up for a time, it didn't break his spirit. He came back to the Flathead and started anew, and with the help of good neighbors and friends, and his sons, it wasn't too long before he was back in the cow business again.

In later years, Herman was a Director of the Conrad National Bank at Kalispell, one of the main backs in the country today. He also was a Director of the Portland Loan Company. He had a lively interest in the people and affairs of the country. At one time he operated a cafe in Plains, and toward the sunset years of his life when they lived in Elmo, he and Vergie ran a hotel.

L.G.'s wife, Thelma Johnson, came to the Flathead from North Dakota on July 4, 1910. Her stop was at Polson, on the south shore of Flathead Lake. Her father and H.S. Hanson started the Security State Bank of Polson, still operating, in 1910. L.G. said that Thelma came with the barbwire and mustard, and he always called her a newcomer. She went through school in Polson, took nurse's training in Minneapolis, and she and L.G. were married May 30, 1925. They had 2 daughters, Beverly and Marilyn. L.G. died December 6, 1959, and Thelma is living in Phoenix, Arizona.

Coke Herman was packing up in Glacier Park when he met his future wife, Louise. She was from Huchinson, Minnesota, a school teacher who had taught for a year in Huchinson before coming west. It was the summer of 1923 that Lou came to western Montana and got a job in Glacier Park. They were married on December 31, 1927. They had one son, Leigh, who is ranching in the Niarada area with his wife, Judy, and four children, making up the fifth generation of Hermans in this part of the country.

Coke passed away on July 31, 1943, and Lou is living in Hot Springs, Montana. It is interesting to note that L.G. and Coke Herman discovered the Flathead Mine, north of Niarada, which is still operating. They were throwing rocks at some horses, and one particularly interesting rock they took home, had it assayed, and discovered it held much silver. Herman received $25,000 for this discovery from the Anaconda Copper Company, as this discovery was on their land.

Both John and Vergie passed away in 1942. Remarkably agile all his life, John took part in the roundups and brandings for many years after he was an old man. He lived a rich, full life, knowing much happiness but also much sadness; knowing wealth and failure, and having the respect of his friends and neighbors who said, "Johnny Herman was a gentleman, and he would never say die."

John & Vergie Herman

John standing at cow camp

ROLEY

We were used to seeing the old man shuffle past our place everyday, stooped and shaky and slow, pushing his walking cane ahead of him to help steady his tired old legs. And always either at his side or at his heels, that old black dog, equally slow, but steady, his mouth open, tongue lolling as he carefully made his way, now and then looking to the side but never leaving his master to investigate things that had interested him when he was younger.

The old dog was named Roley, and he was a Shepard cross of some kind, black with white legs and chest and a white snip on his nose. He was overly-fat, as some old dogs are, and he almost waddled as he walked. The old man had had this pardner since it was a pup and where one went the other went. Roley stayed in the house, either following the old man on his shaky legs, or laying quietly and following him with this eyes. For he knew about every step the old man was going to take, and he didn't bother to get up and follow. He knew so many words too, and his master only had to speak to him softly, informing the old dog of his plans and the dog seemed to understand.

His favorite time of day, other than eating, was to follow the old man to the mailbox to get the daily paper, and mail, if there was ever any mail, which was seldom because the old fellow had no relatives or anyone to send him any mail.

We watched them daily, and knew they were both all right. If we missed them coming, we caught them on the way home because they were in front of our house for such a long time, slowly making their way. The old man knew we, or some of the other neighbors, would pick up his paper, but this seemed to be a trip he looked forward to, probably one of the few diversions he had to what must have been a humdrum kind of life.

He also knew that we would take him to town whenever he needed to go, which was seldom. But he had to go now and then for supplies, or at least he could send a list with one of the neighbors if he needed something. He had a telephone… we were all grateful for that. If he was ever late on his trip to the mailbox, we could call and check on him. But this seldom happened; you could almost set the clock by his daily trips.

Then one day the old man was late and there was no answer when we tried to call him. About the time we were going to his cabin to check on him, he appeared on the narrow dirt road, shuffling along, slower than ever, head down, shoulders stooped, and that cane reaching out ahead of him. Alone. No dog. We immediately knew that the dog had either taken sick, or worse yet, had died.

We met the old fellow at the gate, and he told us: Roley had died the day before, just never woke up from his nap. The old man's eyes were sad as he told us. And he said, "I don't know what I'll do without him, but I'm glad he went before I did." And he said, "Have you ever heard of the dog over in For Benton that met the train every day for 5 or 6 years, looking for his master? His name was Shep, and his owner was a sheepherder that had died and been taken away on the railroad. That dog never gave up, he met that train every day. Of course the people in town tried to catch him but they never could. But they did feed him all these years, and then one day when the dog was old and probably couldn't hear or see so well, he was killed by a train. Now, maybe that dog forgot eventually what he was looking for as some say, but I don't think so. I think he knew till the end what he was waiting for."

The old man wiped his eyes, and he said, "Now you see what I mean? When Roley died, I understood what had happened and I knew he was gone. But ol' Roley, he wouldn't know if I went first, what happened or why, and he'd just keep lookin' for me and he'd grieve himself to death." He bade us goodbye and walked slowly into the mailbox before we could say much except "I'm sorry."

It wasn't but a couple months later that the old man didn't go for the newspaper, and after watching for him for a short time, we decided we'd better check. So we walked up the road, almost knowing what had happened, and sure enough, the old fellow had died, just looked like he went to sleep while sitting in his old rocking chair. Roley hadn't had to wait very long before his pardner joined him.

It's too bad the old man couldn't have been buried beside his friend, or the other way around. But he was buried in our little cemetery, with only a few neighbors there because no one knew where he came from, or if there was anyone to notify.

And Roley? Well, the old man must have worked for many, many hours, digging in that hard ground to make a grave for his loyal friend, and Roley was buried with only one person in attendance, the only friend he knew. There was a little mound over the grave, and what looked to be the end of an apple box, with Roley's name painted on it, set into the ground at the end of the mound.

ED LANE

Ed Lane raised Palomino and Appaloosa horses in the Jocko Valley. I bought a young palomino stallion from him in 1941. Mr. Lane sold to buyers who wanted beautiful horses for parades, circus events, rodeos, and even to movie producers. In 1941, a colorful, halter trained 2 year old would bring $150, and some sold for a lot more.

My long-time friend, Rosie, went with me when I picked out my young stallion. Ed Lane was in his 70's then, and still actively involved in shows and rodeo. We were able to ride a couple of his Appaloosa horses. He was such an interesting man.

He raised purebred Hereford cattle with his herd numbering 200 head. He put up Alfalfa hay for winter, and the Jocko was known for lush fields of hay, and pastures of green grass.

Ed Lane rode with Teddy Roosevelt's Rough Riders during the Spanish American War that began in 1898. When he was out of the service he joined the James and Younger Wild West show. He rode saddle broncs and played a Scout in Younger's "Great Train Robbery", and also rode in some of Buffalo Bill's shows.

Mr. Lane and his newly acquired partner, Gray Scott, started providing horses for wild west shows, and the Ringling Brothers Circus. Training young horses was a major part of his life as a rancher.

Ed Lane was born in Pennsylvania in 1867 and died November 10, 1946 at the age of 79. He was posthumously inducted into the Montana Cowboy Hall Of Fame in January of 2014.

Rosie Swisher Ed Lane Fay Poloson

Fay & Ed Lane

Ed Lane's Palominos

LADDIE CAME HOME

Laddie at the Big Bend Ranch

Laddie was a Collie, that we knew, but only from his looks. I have forgotten where he came from, but remember that he was not wanted by whoever had him at the time. So, we took him, a small, lanky pup that was full of play and activity. He made himself at home on the ranch, and was with us whenever we went riding, or working stock, feeding, or whatever was to be done. He was full of ambition and he thought he was helping. He was not a good dog around livestock. Mainly he trotted around, head and tail up, looking and appearing to laugh as he either got in the way, or turned the cattle the wrong direction. Or stood in the gate we meant for the cows to go through, and blocked their path. But he was such a friendly, lovable dog, and a good watchdog. So, we kept him. And the longer we kept him, the more fond we became of big old golden Laddie. Because he was big, and kept growing until he was big as a Guernsey calf.

We never took Laddie with us when we went anywhere, so he knew it was his duty to stay home and "take care of things." He never tried to follow a vehicle, or if we told him to stay home, he wouldn't follow the saddlehorses either. Laddie minded well, and he didn't seem to care as long as he could frolic and show off when we were at home.

One day we went to town, arriving home late that night after dark. Laddie didn't come to meet us, and we wondered about it, but thought sure he would be back from wherever he had gone to investigate whatever it was that he liked to pursue.

But morning came, still no Laddie. Days passed, and he still didn't show up, so we finally gave him up. We had advised the neighbors that our dog was missing, but no one had seen him. We thought, either he was dead someplace out in the field, or possibly someone had driven up and he followed them, or even got in a car with someone. He loved everyone and trusted everyone.

It was quiet and sad without our good dog, and we never stopped wondering what happened to him. Had we come upon his body somewhere, at least it would have been a relief to know what had happened to him. But not a sign. This was in the early spring of the year.

Bill's sister and brother-in-law had come for a couple of weeks' visit in August, and when work was done at home, we'd take a drive someplace to show them the country. This day we went over to the Bill & Ada Gould Ranch on Round Butte. They raised buffalo and Quarter Horses, and like our ranch, did all their work with saddle or work horses. Real friendly people, they loved company, and enjoying showing the buffalo and horses to anyone who was interested.

We had fun that afternoon. Bill harnessed the team, and took us for a ride on the hay wagon, to look at the buffalo. This was an exciting time for all of us, especially so, since one big old buffalo cow was on the prod, and charged the wagon. We all hustled to the other side, and Bill whipped the team up and got us out of her way.

Imagine how city people would feel over such a close call! This was the first live buffalo they had ever seen.

Finally it was time to leave, so we headed for home in our car. It was just starting to get dark. We had gone a couple miles down the road, when we saw a dog trotting along beside the road. He turned as we neared and Bill said, "That looks like Laddie." So he pulled alongside the dog, I opened the door to talk to the dog, but before I could say a word, he jumped in! And it was Laddie! He was thin, ragged and footsore, but it was our Laddie. I don't know who was the happiest, Bill and I, or that poor old tired-out dog.

Where had he been? How long had he traveled? We will never know. Later, in talking to Goulds, they told us the dog had been to their place a day or two before, and they had fed him. Bill said it seemed the dog was traveling, and just wanted to stop over, rest, and get something to eat. Then he disappeared. We always wondered where he was when we were at Gould's, where we had missed him.

So Laddie's lost months will always be a mystery, but things continued as always once Laddie got home again, fattened up and became his old self. He was with us until he died of old age. I often wished he could have talked. What a tale that old Collie dog would probably have told! We are sure someone picked him up and probably took him a long ways from home. Obviously he had traveled far because his feet were so sore it was difficult for him to walk on the graveled road. His hair was matted and he was so this his bones almost rattled, so he had to have come a long ways. But the main thing was, Laddie came home!

Fay & Bill had recently sold their Big Bend Ranch and moved to the Ronan place. I think Laddie went back to the Big Bend place and waited for them. Finally, when they didn't come home, he set out for the Ronan place.

A DOG'S LIFE

Barney & White Tail by the old Poloson mailbox. Early 1940's.

Barney looking for rabbits

Barney patrolling the pasture

Well, I don't know much about writin' stories, especially stories about myself, but as the saying goes, I'll try anything once. So here's a long tale of a dog.

I was born on the first of March, and guess if I'd been born just a little sooner, I wouldn't have seen daylight. For all my little brothers and sisters were killed. But I was lucky, as I usually am, and the boss's wife ran onto me before he did. So she goes and tells her daughter there's a pup in the dog-house and if she wants him to take him to the chicken-house where no one will be apt to look for dogs, or pups. So Fay went and got me, and with my anxious mother following, took me to the chicken-house. There weren't no chickens there, for which I was glad, though I guess I wouldn't have known a chicken from a falling star at the time. Anyhow, I stayed there for a long time, rolled up in a ball to keep warm, 'cause in them days it was pretty cold, and all I had was my mother and a bed of dried grass to keep me warm. And one night all I had was the grass, 'cause they shut my mother up in the dog-house. Next day she was turned out again, and boy was I tickled to see her.

Well, later on, my eyes opened up a little and I could see a few feet in front of my nose, not so far though. Then finally they opened wide and was I surprised to see funny looking creatures, *so* much bigger than me, walking on two legs, and picking me up, and boy was I scared. I used to see, or hear them coming in my house, and would back up in a corner and sorta growl, and then I'd let a loud bark, probably not so loud compared to what I can do now, and at the time they told me I said "Bip, bip, bip!" Kind of sissified bark for even a little feller.

Soon I was walking around out in the sunshine, and did I like that. They used to call me to try to get me to the house, but no siree, I wouldn't leave that old chicken-house for nothing. It was home and safety to me, an' I wasn't gonna leave it, no sir! But soon I did. And wasn't sorry either. And finally the time came when I didn't give a darn about the old place any more. They'd always let me in when I'd cry at the door, and it sure was nice an' warm in the house with all the people. And when my mother weaned me, the folks took me as their own. So I didn't miss her so much, then finally I just forgot about her.

When summer came, I was kinda lonesome, for Fay was always out with the horses, but then I liked to stay in the house with her mother. I was scared of horses. Gee, were they big compared to me, and I wasn't gonna have anything to do with any of 'em. But finally Fay would keep on a-callin' me, and I'd go a little ways, and the horse never hurt me, so I soon got to following her for short distances. But boy, was that tiresome on the legs. I don't know how a horse can go so far and so fast. It sure was tough on me. But ole Pal, the horse I always followed, he was long-legged and tough too, so it was okay for him to go a long ways. At first I didn't care much for him, but after we went together for awhile, boy that old horse got to mean almost as much to me as he does to Fay. An' that's a-plenty, 'cause she sure loves that horse. She used to, when I'd get so tired it was impossible for me to keep up, she'd call me, reach down, and when I'd whine and jump up with my front feet on Pal's leg, as high up as I could reach, she's grab me by the neck (sometimes I'd cry 'cause it sure pulled my hair and hide) and lift me up in front of her on Pal. I sure liked that. It was swell to go so fast and not hafta use your own power. But she said I moved around too much and scratched up her saddle. When she got her new Porter, she only let me ride a couple times. Till she notice the little toe-tail marks all over the front of it, I guess. Maybe I should've kept still, but it's kinda scary sometimes when a horse is goin' downhill or turns quick.

When I was about ten months old, I was sleeping by the warm stove, and saw Fay dressed up real warm, and I knew then she was gonna ride. She got her bridle and caught ol' Pal, and seemed in a hurry. Sorta worried, I guessed, and then I heard her talking about some mares and baby colts out in the hills. Then I knew what was wrong. It hadn't got too bad weather then, but those little fellers and their mothers have a hard time anyway in the winter. And so we took out hunting, up the south hills and to the Diamond, where the Wild Horse Corral is. The Diamond, so called because it is a big bare side hill in the shape of a diamond, surrounded in trees. And in the SW corner is, or rather was a good big corral, in fact two of them. One was a fairly good-sized one and the other, down in the tall trees, was just a little one, for putting the wild horses they wanted to keep in I'd say. And there was a big wing, running out across the diamond, to run the horses in. It got wider as you went out on the ridge, and they said the mouth was two miles wide. Might be just a story, but you know, where there's smoke there's fire, they say. And this wing narrowed down till it ran right into the biggest corral gate. I'd like to've seen them runnin' wild horses in there, years and years ago. Now the old corral are 'most all fell down, and the wing is altogether down. Just a memory of the old west that used to be, and I bet lots of old-time cowboys could tell lots about that old horse-running business.

Well, to go on with my story, we didn't find the horses that day. Nor the next, nor the day after that. And it was pretty cold too. By the time we'd get home, all of us were about froze. But we never gave up, till it started to snow so hard we couldn't hardly go out without freezing in the first hour. So stayed close to home, and she worried. I did some, but never thought so much about it. Then finally the snow and cold weather let up a bit, but by then there was snow about two feet deep all the way up toward the Wild Horse Corral, and boy, was that tough going! It was all I could do to get up there, and I saw old Pal was always pouring sweat and blowing like a Norther when we made the top. He used to go up, I remembered, before the snow; he'd go clear to the top without stopping. But not now. He had to stop several times, and I could see it was hard on him to travel even with rests. He wanted to go back home. So did I, and she did too, but wasn't thinking of us. She was thinking 'bout her horses. There was two bunches missing, the mares, stallion and colts, and some yearlings and a few more in another bunch. She never worried so much about the others, it was the mares that bothered her. Thinking of those little fellers digging gin the snow for feed, freezing their legs and noses, crusts of snow on their little backs — and the mares, feeding their colts and most of them going to have colts in the spring too. That was a double chore for them, besides feeding themselves. But I guess the stallion was the boss of where they went, where we finally found them after the snow started to melt. But that's getting ahead of the story. I'll tell you about the loneliest time I think I ever had. We'd been hunting for a couple weeks, I guess. Me and Pal were both getting pretty skinny and run-down. And his back and legs were getting mighty tired and sore. But he never complained, just kept going, wherever she wanted him to go, whatever speed she wanted him to take. Sometimes, we'd come down those hills on a trot, when she was getting pretty cold, and wanted to get home before it got too cold in the evening. For about a month, you can imagine what it'd be like, going up for about three miles, through snow stirrup-deep, where she had to hold her feet up high so's not to freeze them in the stirrups, and going on across the ridges, where the wind was blowing, and freezing everything it hit. Going over rock-piles that she wouldn't have thought of crossing if it were uncovered so she could see what they were like. Heading for home at the last minute, when she was just too cold to go any farther. One day I remember she went back east of home, for about eight or nine miles, through that deep and cold snow, down canyons and across ridges, when finally Pal was almost too tired to go on, she saw some horses, and with hopes high, went to them, only to find some range horses of someone else's.

The next day we went again. The snow was getting sort of wet by then, and was sure hard for me to go through, 'cause it balled up all over me. Don't know how Pal made it, but he hasn't got such long hair as I've got. His legs are trim and not much hair on them, long hair anyway. But lots of times his feet balled up and almost threw him. Of course in the deep snow, there wasn't much danger of being thrown by balled-up feet, but when we'd go down the logging road, right close to home, it wasn't so good.

We started out that day anyhow, and it was awfully cold, colder than it had been since we'd been traveling. And the snow was wetter than usual, so she got a long ways ahead of me. But no sir, I wasn't gonna turn around and go home. I ain't no quitter, and I figured maybe I better be there in case something should happen to them. Don't know why, but just thought I should be. Probably I couldn't do anything to help, but that never entered my head. I guess she was clear to the top of the hill by the time I was half-way up, and boy was it hard going too. All I could do to make it. I though too turning back but didn't. And finally I tracked Pal to an old cabin. I saw where she'd got off the horse, and gone in and built a fire. But guess it smoked her out. She said later there was no stove-pipe, but she was almost froze and had to build a fire or freeze. She said it never done much good, but it helped some. Anyhow, I smelled the tracks and couldn't see her anywhere. It never occurred to me to look around and see where they went from there. I just figured they'd disappeared in the air or somethin'. So I sat down and let a mournful howl and whined a little. Then listened. And I thought I heard her call. So I howled again. And sure enough, I did hear her, and she whistled to me too. So I howled a few more times, and going around the cabin, saw where the horse's tracks went on east of there, down the canyon up the other side. It was getting dark then, so I thought I'd best get a move on. I went as fast as I could, stopping now and then to cry a little and lick my legs, chew the ice off my legs and belly, and rest a little. I should've turned and gone straight home from there, but didn't. She circled around the ridge, and headed back, and guess she figured I'd cut across and meet her, but not. I circled too, right in Pal's tracks. And then I knew she was going home. And when I finally struggled and fought through the snow to the logging road, I was so tired I thought I couldn't make it on, and cold too. But it was dark and I knew they'd worry about me some, so I went on fast as I could make it, and about eight, I got home and whined to get in. She was there already, and had been for an hour or maybe more. It was pitch dark then, and boy was I glad to get home, and get warmed up, I never would wish myself such a lonely trip again, howling on the hill, kinda scared of coyotes, and wondering where I was, when, and if I'd ever get home…

Next day of course we were out again. And so on till the snow started to go off, and then about the time it started to warm up, here came almost blizzard, and we all worried some more about them horses. When the snow let up, someone was coming up the road and saw some horses in place southwest of home, down out of the timber, but she never thought of it being her horses. It was almost impossible for it to be them, she thought. But she went over one morning. I never went this trip, just got the facts from stories going around that noon. I sure was disappointed when they shut me up, and would have followed, but wasn't sure what way the horse went. So I had to stay home and wonder when they'd be back. It was about noon when they did come, with no horses, because she had misunderstood and gone up the ridge, and to a bare place on top, when the horses were on the other side of a the fence. She would've hunted some more, gone down the ridge, and if she'd done that, would have found the horses, but she got all full of snow and a cold wind started to blow, so she came home to dry off. It seems she started up to cross a drift, and couldn't make it. I've seen Pal do that lots, and he'd rear up and whirl and go back the way he came. He just couldn't get thru some of the deep places, but it took pretty deep drift to stop him at that. And tired as he usually was at the top of the ridges, it's a wonder he could get thru any of the deep drifts. Not many horses would or could go on like that one. He's one in a thousand, I'll tell you. Never give up and never slow up, that horse. Well, he couldn't make it through one drift, so went around and started up where it was a little sheltered by a cliff. That was okay and they'd have made it if he hadn't stepson on a rock under the snow and fell. And he was too tired and weak from a month's fighting snow to struggle much. She was scared half to death, in fact she said she was more scared and worried than she'd ever been before or since. For Pal fell with his back downhill, and it doesn't take long for a horse to die that way. His back was down against a log, sort of a rotten limb holding him, and he wouldn't fight to get up. She uncinched the saddle and struggled through almost waist-deep snow, to his head where she slapped his nose to make him try to get away. She pulled his head around to try and get him to make at least a try, but a groan and hard breathing was all she could get from him. Luckily the rotten limb gave 'way, or that horse would be there yet. The limb broke and he slid on top of the snow, to a couple little trees, where he stopped. She followed and pulled his head around downhill. He slid on the snow, of course, till he was sorta facing downhill, and then he gave a lunge and got up, where he stood trembling and panting, head lowered and blood on his stomach where a limb on the rotten log had scratched him. But it wasn't bad, and she saddled him and they went on. Guess that was when she really breathed a sigh of relief, when they'd started on again. As much as she thinks of that horse, if he hadn't got up again, I don't think she would have either. By then they were both full of snow, and when they got to the top of the ridge, over the drift there was an ice wind blowing, and she figured best they go home. So later that day she got straight facts as to where the horses were, and we took out again. This time I went 'cause she wasn't going far. If this wasn't her horses, she'd give up till it got warmer and Pal was stronger. He was worth more to her than all the horses that were gone, and she'd rather keep him with her than all the horses in Montana. Well anyway, we went through a gate and up a little hill, and when I heard her holler "Gold Dust" I knew she'd found her horses, 'cause Gold Dust is that pretty little shiny Palomino she has. And Pal's ears went up, and his step quickened. I run up and smell a little colt's heels and almost got kicked. Never could figure why they kick at me when I'm just trying to find out how they are. The little ones were just a little thin, shaggy as could be, but they looked okay. The mares is what looked bad, even though the stallion had tried to get them to good feed, they were all thin as rails. I think that was one of her happiest days, when she got them horses heading for home, and feed. I was pretty glad too, 'cause it ended those hard days in the snow, and I know if she'd gone again I'd have to seek away, or get shut up. And I sure hated to get shut in when that bay horse was going anywhere. Anyway, we got the mares and colts home, and safely on the feed grounds, where they started to pick up right away. Then when it warmed up we took out after the yearlings and their bunch. If they'd made through so far, she reasoned, they were okay, but we'd try to find them anyway. Then the boss went out one day when she stayed home, and it was so foggy, and getting late too. He heard a bell when he was at the Wild Horse Corral and since a white horse in our bunch packed a bell, he thought that was our bunch. And it was. Next day he rode a half-broke bay colt and Fay took Pal, and my mother and I went along. We were about lost in the fog, couldn't see more than ten feet ahead, and I guess they just went along the sorts of the timber and to the top of the hill, where we could see tree-tops and nothing else to let us know we weren't on top of the world. 'Cause all around us, just like a lake, was fog. We could see the sky, a bright blue and sure pretty, the tree-tops right by us, and that foggy lake. It was a sight, and nice and warm too. We could hear the bell every once in a while, and went down into the fog again, expecting to follow the ridge down to the horses. I saw two coyotes, seemingly gentle, but when the saw us they sure went. They had been only a little way from us, sitting up staring rudely, but you should've seen 'em go when Ma an' me took out after 'em. Scared I guess. Cowards. Well, we went on down and would've passed the horses I guess if the colt hadn't smelled or heard them or somethin' an' took out. Nothin' could stop him so we just followed and finally heard a horse call, and out of the fog came all the ones we were hunting. They didn't look bad, guess the bunch grass was good and range horses can paw for it.

Well all the horses were accounted for, and the rest of the winter was pretty easy for us. Pal was out eating hay and she always fed him oats a couple times a day, but he didn't pick up much till she turned him out to rest in the spring and rode other horses. He looks swell now. I'd like it if fine if she would catch him and ride him, but she says he deserves a rest for a while, and for a change. He's had three years of hard work, she says, and she knows now he's the best horse she's ever had, ever will have, or ever know or see. I agree with her somehow. You would too if you knew that horse like we do.

Well, spring was pretty good, only kinda rainy after a while. But at first, it was nice out, sunshine and not very much cold weather. It was on a pretty swell day that we started out for the mailbox, Fay and Pal, Pete, another pup, and me. Well, about a mile down, I took after a rabbit an' boy could he go! But I was just about two jumps behind, and not paying attention to anything except Mr. Rabbit, when all of a sudden — whooey! I was fallin' an' fallin' and when I'd try to catch myself, or hang onto somethin' my feet would slip and I'd just keep on, fallin' down and down till finally I hit with a thud that 'most shed every tooth and hair, and sorta stunned me too. It seemed I fell about a mile down, but I learned later it was only 65 feet — did I say *only*?

Well, anyhow, it was some experience, and I bet there's not more than one dog in a couple million can say they spent three days sixty-five feet down in the ground, 'cause it was three days before Fay found me. And was she glad to see me. I thought I heard old Pal walking, and couldn't hardly believe my ears, so I kept still till I heard her call.

Then boy, you should've seen and heard me, jumping up, howling and crying. Boy, I was glad. Had begun to think no one was ever gonna find me, but I hadn't give up all hopes. I thought someone would run onto me, but there was no way to send any signals, even if I knew how. I wanted her to stay with me, but no, she got on Pal and for the longest time I could hear him running toward home, I guess it was. And in just a little while I heard him again, coming back toward my well, and this time she had some meat for me, and dropped it to me. When that mean dropped on the bottom of that well, you could hear it a mile and a half, I betcha. But I sure as glad to be able to get some grub of some kind, 'cause gee, I was a hungry pup. she was callin' me an' tellin' me it would be all right, and I was eatin' a bite of meat an' jumpin', tryin' to catch a hold of somethin', but the sides of that old well were ice all the way from top to bottom, so I couldn't get anything to catch onto. Then just a little while I heard a car, and here came the boys, with a long rope. They put a loop in it and let it down, but I was so tickled and in a hurry when I jumped for the loop I hit it wrong and it closed. So to all our disappointment, they pulled it up again. But next time they let a loop down I jumped right into it and it felt swell to be pulled up to air and daylight again. I tried to thank the boys, then sees Fay and Pal a-waitin' for me on the other side of the fence, and boy oh boy, did I scoot under that ol' fence like a chicken with a coyote on its tail, however that is, and jumped up on her, and Pal. Then we all pulled out for home, me goin' 'way ahead to see how things were, and sorta get things read for the rest of them, clear the road and all, you know. Well, I was welcomed a-plenty an' can tell all you pups and dogs about my adventures that would fill a book, as they often tell me, if I could write good enough to write a book. Well, I can honestly tell you, hereafter I stay away from deep places, an' above all I stay away from the location of that hole I was in. Would not want to fall in that again, for rabbit or money.

Guess I've sorta run things into a horse, dog, and girl story, haven't I? But my life wouldn't fill up a page very interesting all alone. Oh, yep, I know I've had lotsa adventures, but I gotta be modest and let someone else share my fame, you see. I never was one to take all the credit; I just want most of it.

SHELLEY

Shellie

Fay with Shellie and a pal at the Big Bend Ranch

Fay & Shellie taking a vacation

I've heard it said that a person is lucky to have one outstanding horse in a lifetime, I wonder if the same doesn't hold true of dogs. Sure, I've had some good dogs that I liked, and some not so good dogs that I also liked. Maybe one or two I strongly disliked.

But, the one I think of most often, the one I loved and missed the most, was Shelley Of Wiltshire, a little tri-colored Shetland Sheepdog. She went with me all the time, whether it was checking the horses on a cold, snowy day, or a trip to town.

Bill and I met her in Missoula, this little bundle of fur that was to be our friend and companion for so many years.

Shelley, my friend, my treasure. If you ever have a Sheltie you'll never want another. Shelley had a bed on the back seat of our car. When we were in Great Falls, we lost her. It wasn't until we heard her barking that it donned on us, we'd shut her in the trunk; whenever we had it opened to unload our suitcases, etc., Shelley would jump in, curl up, and fall asleep. Shelley and her pal, Eddie, got into a fight in our hotel room that night. Quite a disturbance, but we didn't have to leave the hotel.

When our friends, Jan & Lu, were visiting, our horseback ride was too long for Shelley, so I picked her up and she rode behind me on Jule Bar. She was a Jule Bar passenger many times over the years that we had her.

When we were riding up in the Mission Range, Shelley fell off a log and into the creek. I rescued her; she rode horseback the rest of that trip. That night, as we headed home, we stopped to put the trailer dust door on. Shelley got out, and we didn't notice that she was not on her bed on the back seat. Several miles later we discovered an empty bed! We turned around, drove back, and Shelley was waiting by the old Sloan Bridge.

The next day, she was run over by a horse at the Pony Palace "Roping." She survived that but was lost again on our trip up to the Whitman Place; we'd gone to move the mares to another pasture. Again, Shelley's barking led us to her. The tone of her bark depended on the situation; was she in trouble, excited, scared, or angry.

Shellie loved all the action at the Pony Palace. She would sit on the table in the Pony Palace lunch room, or she'd lay underneath. It was hard for her to be still, so she thought she should be part of the action, and ended up under a horse's feet. She wasn't hurt, and she went on to watch the show. Shellie enjoyed the horse activities more than most of the spectators did.

Shelley's end came quietly. She just went to sleep.

TIPPY

I got Tippy in March of 1998. She was a wonderful companion, kept an eye on the miniature horses, and my place. Tippy loved to watch TV, especially rodeos and she was fascinated by the bull riding events.

My niece, Grace, was visiting; she is an early riser and wanted to watch TV. But, she couldn't figure out how to turn my TV on. Tippy kept staring at her, "what on earth is wrong with this person? They can't even turn the TV on?"

WILD HORSE ISLAND ROUNDUP

Western Horseman June 1965

Wild Horse Island Flathead Lake

Bill & Fay having lunch on Wild Hose Island

Corralled horses at Elmo   Unloading at Elmo

Going to Wild Hors   On the way to Wild Horse Island
Island on Hidges' Barge

Guy Clatterbuck Napping

Barge load of hay for horses on the Island

Neil DeGolier, Mechanic, Bud Lake, Oral Zumwalt, & Guy Clatterbuck

Unloading at Elmo

Unloading at Elmo

Horses on the Island

Corralled horses on the Island

Up in northwestern Montana in *big sky country,* lies a clear, beautiful lake known as Flathead, named for the Flathead Indian tribe. And about 28 miles long and 15 miles wide, this lake has furnished entertainment for tourists from far and wide with its boating, water skiing, and fishing; and the beauty along its shorelines has been the subject of photography and enjoyment by people from all walks of life.

This area is also well-known for its farms, ranches, friendly towns, and the delicious sweet cherries grown so abundantly along the lake's shores.

Another attraction of the Flathead Lake is Wild Horse Island, situated in the southwestern part of the lake, about a mile offshore at the closest point. Not too much is known of the history of the island except by the old-timers and people living in the area. However, it is of interest to passers-by who marvel at this unusual and picturesque island in what is known as Montana's *paradise.*

At one time there were many homesteads on the island, which has about 3,000 acres. When the country was opened to homesteading in 1910, the island was included, and among the first homesteaders were L.E. Thurber, Roy Torkinson, a Mr. Norberg, Mr. Powers, and the famous German photographer, Herman Schnitzmeyer.

In 1915, the government sold land in the lake area as villa sites, and Col. A.A. White of St. Paul purchased several sites on Wild Horse Island.

Judge Padbury and Mr. Penwell owned land on the island, as well as did the state university and the Indian Department. Penwell operated Hiawatha Lodge on the east end for some time, and ran a bunch of horses on the island.

On the west shore of the Lake near Rollins was the Clatterbuck Guest Ranch, owned and operated by Mr. and Mrs. Guy Clatterbuck and son, Ted, and a very popular resort at the time. It was to Clatterbucks that Dr. J.C. Burnett and his wife came from New York to spend their vacations during World War II. Dr. Burnett was a retired osteopath, and his wife was an heiress to a roller bearing corporation. Doc, as he was called, became interested in the island, and decided he would own his unique land. Money was of no concern to the Burnetts, but the big job would be to locate the owners and heirs of the island. So they hired A.L. (Lloyd) Helmer of Polson and set out to gather the necessary information. After a year's travel and investigation, the papers were finally in order; Doc was able to buy every foot of the island, and only then would be put his money down.

This was a great new undertaking for Doc, and he spent considerable time on the island. Mrs. Burnett was an elderly lady, and the wild west held little appeal to her, so she spent but one summer there.

Doc had hired Guy Clatterbuck as superintendent of the island. Guy was a well-known and popular cowboy in the country. And so began the years of enjoyment (and hard work) that went with Wild Horse Island. Many trips back and forth in a boat were sometimes pleasant, sometimes highly dangerous, because Flathead Lake in a storm can be mighty wild.

The first thing done was to hire two more cowboys, Bud Lake and Bob Gray, and clear all the horses from the island. A few of these horses Ted Clutterbuck broke, and the rest were sold. Then Doc proceeded to buy mares from here and there over the country and move them to the island by barge, to be turned loose on the range. He bought a very classic purebred Arabian stallion in Arizona and turned him loose with the mares. This horse was used to being pampered, and his life was difficult those first few years as a range horse, especially in winter.

His next step was to buy Riskulus, a Thoroughbred stallion in Kentucky, for $33,000. Riskulus was sired by Stimulus, by Ultimus, and had an enviable record on the track at the time. From 1933 through 1936 he won $32,000 on the racetrack, a lot of money in those days of small purses. He won at many of the best tracks, and set a track record at Santa Anita for the mile and an eighth as a four-year-old.

Riskulus was cared for in his own pen and barn on the island, but was bred to only a few mares. He was shipped back to Kentucky for the winter, and the following spring Doc shipped him back to Montana and gave him to Bud Lake. Doc had almost lost interest in the horses by that time, and his interest in the island was also fast waning. Other businesses and investments in all parts of the world claimed his attention.

The deer were plentiful on Wild Horse Island, and every fall about hunting season they would swim from shore to Cromwell, a small island between shore and Wild Horse, and then on to the main island. Many times in the fall over 400 deer would roam the island. Then mountain sheep, two ewes and a ram, were turned loose on the island, to begin what would amount to well over 100 sheep in a fairly short time. This was ideal country for the sheep — dry, rough, and with timbered draws to hide in.

Doc loved animals, and the deer, mountain sheep, and wild horses on the island were a great source of entertainment for him. Guy had found him a good saddle horse, a big sorrel from the New Lynch ranch at Plains, half-Thoroughbred and half-Percheron. Doc and his outfit weighed around 275 pounds, so it took more than just an average horse to carry him over that rough country. He was fond of Chief, though he rode the horse hard when he did ride him. Riding a form-fitting saddle, he loved to chase horses with the cowboys. He would ride up high on one of the ridges, throw old Chief his head, and go whooping and yelling down the sidehill, as they said, "like a pebble down a well." It would chill you, visioning the horse falling and the pair of them rolling clear to the lake! Fortunately Chief was extra good on his feet.

Doc was a kind-hearted, generous, and friendly man, and this big new, open country was to his liking at the time, and perhaps it gave him some of the most fun he had in his life.

A deer that stayed around the main house was thought to be a pet of the Penwell children. She gathered all her friends and relatives, and they moved in to eat the saddle horses' hay and grain. Every time the horses were fed, Dinah and her pals were right there for their share.

Doc decided he should have a horse breaker on the island, so Guy hired Bill Haynes who was rodeoing at the time, and the big chore began. Doc wanted the mares broke, and although most of them were never touched again, Bill broke those old wild mares to ride. That was the summer Mrs. Burnett was on the island, and she and Doc spent long hours in the jeep up at the horse corrals watching Bill work with the horses. It was all fun to Doc, and many times he would follow Bill along the lakeshore or sidehills in his jeep, banging on the sides and whooping to stampeded the horse. This didn't go over so well with Bill at first, but he finally realized it was the way Doc wanted it, and after all, he was paying the bills and they were his horses. So let him have his fun! There was also a mule on the island, and Doc insisted on Bill riding it for the amusement of his friends. Finally the mule quit bucking which ended that.

Doc liked to kiss his horses on the nose, and many times barely escaped a hoof on his chin. He wanted to ride all the horses, too; and finally there was one little bay mare that got pretty gentle, so one day Doc rode her out to help gather horses. They came for the corrals on a run as usual, this time Doc right in their midst. The first thing Bill knew, Doc was on his back on the ground, a foot hung in his stirrup. Luckily the little mare stood while Bill quietly took Doc loose. The big man was trying to run his horse into the corral, set her up, and step off "like you cowboys do."

The horses were mainly sorrels with white markings, with almost all the young ones at least half-Arabian. The colts were gelded in the fall with Bill doing the veterinarian chores. Many a roundup was held with Guy, Bill, and me doing most of the riding. Sometimes horses from the island were used, but mainly special horses were brought from shore by barge.

It took a good horse to travel this country and successfully gather the stock that had run wild all their lives, the case with most of them. The terrain was rough, steep, and rocky; the horses were wily, smart, tough and used to the country.

Some favorite horses on these island roundups were Bill's Iron Horse, a brown Thoroughbred that only knew the word *go;* Night, a black horse I usually rode was a Thoroughbred-Morgan-Arabian cross, not a very pretty horse, but what a horse runner — he loved it and he seemed to know just what those horses were going to do all the time; Red, a son of Riskulus owned by Guy, a big, beautiful sorrel horse that proved himself a top horse on the island; and Eagle, a cream-colored horse raised by us, just a young horse but tough and willing. Generally this work was too hard for an unseasoned horse so mainly the older, tough using horses were taken to the island. Sand and Chief, two of the island horses were sometimes used, as well as a few of the gentler ones Bill had broke to ride, if extra riders were on hand.

In 1954, there were over 100 range horses on the island, and Doc decided to sell half of them. At one time he planned to ship them to New York but decided this would be impractical. He sent word to Guy, telling him which horses he wanted saved, and the roundup began that fall. A crew built corrals, fences, and a wing to the shoreline where the horses were to be loaded on a barge.

Riding on this last roundup were Guy Clatterbuck and Bill and myself. Special care was to be given to get every horse in the corrals this time, and the best saddle horses were taken to the island. Hodge's Barge from Polson was hired, and it was a real thrill, riding from Polson to the island, about a three-hour trip along the quiet lake. High sides had been built on the big flat bed of the barge which was complete with living quarters.

This was truly an unforgettable experience, gathering the horses, cutting them out, turning those back on the island that were to stay, and loading the rest on the barge — 49 head of them, and three saddle horses. The wild ones were almost frightened to death, but rode safely to shore near Elmo, where they were corralled and loaded on trucks to go to Missoula and the sale ring.

In the late winter of 1956, reports were made to the humane society that the horses were going hungry on the island, that the snow was too deep, and the grass was gone. Contact was made with Doc, who ordered baled hay flown from Polson to the island. In the opinion of the ranchers in the country, this was very well done, except for one thing; when a horse is eating hay, he must have water. With only grass to eat, snow will replace water. But the horses filled up on fresh, green hay, and could get no water since the lake was frozen over. Consequently most of them died of impaction and this good deed by the humane society backfired. When the Chinooks took the snow a while later, a tragic sight greeted the eyes of visitors to the island. There were four horses and a mule living, and apparently in good shape. Perhaps the others, or most of them, would have survived if left to Nature; who knows?

So the beautiful sorrel horses would run down the ridges and canyons no more, and the glory of Wild Horse Island was gone forever.

Doc came no more. His wife had preceded him in death, and when Doc passed a few years later, the island was put up for sale. But we who rode there can still vision those beautiful horses running wild and free, and remember all the good times we had on the roundups — deer, sheep, and horses, all in a band — where else on earth is there such a setting as this?

THE LAST WILD HORSE ROUND-UP (the RONAN PIONEER February 1982)

In 1954 there were over 100 range horses on Flathead Lake's Wildhorse Island and it was decided by the island owner Dr. J.C. Burnett to remove at least half of them.

So Superintendent of the island Guy Clatterbuck hired some hands to help him accomplish the task. Bill and Fay Haynes, Phillip and Lucille Roullier, Bud Lake, Oral Zumwalt, Roland Anderson, and Bob Gray all combined talents to round up the herd that ranged free over the 2,700 acre island. Corrals and a wing were constructed along the island's north side near the lakeshore and another corral was built on the south side. And then the great roundup began.

As it turned out it was the last for the island. The winter of '56 saw some 50 horses parish because of lack of water.

The horses to be rounded up were mainly sorrels with white markings, with almost all of the young ones at least half-Arabian thanks to Doc's free-ranging and romantic stallion he imported to the island.

Fay Haynes recalled the roundup, "It took a good horse to travel this country and successfully gather the stock that had run wild all their lives, the case with most of them. The terrain was steep, rough and rocky; the horses were smart, tough and used to the country."

Riding on the last roundup were Bill and Fay Haynes and Guy Clatterbuck. Special care was to be given to get every horse in the corrals this time, and the best saddle horses were taken to the island to assist in the roundup.

Mrs. Haynes recounted the roundup in great detail in an article she wrote for the Western Horseman several years ago.

To transport the captured horses to the mainland, Hodges' barge from Polson was hired. "It was a real thrill, riding from Polson to the island, about a three-hour trip along the quiet lake," remembers Fay. "High sides had been built on the big flat bed of the barge which was complete with living quarters."

She said, "This was truly an unforgettable experience, gathering the horses, cutting them out, turning those back on the island that were to stay and loading the rest of the horses onto the barge — 49 head of them and three saddle horses. The wild ones were almost frightened to death but rode safely to shore near Elmo, where they were corralled and loaded onto trucks for Missoula and the sale ring."

After that winter storm took its toll, only four horses and a mule were left. With nostalgia Fay said, "so the beautiful sorrel horses would run down the ridges and canyons no more, and the glory of Wild Horse Island was gone forever."

After Dr. Burnett died, the island was once again for sale. Haynes recalled, "We who rode there can still vision those beautiful horses running wild and free, and remember all the good times we had on the roundups, — sheep, deer, and horses, all in a band — where else on earth is there such as setting as this?" Where indeed.

Today bighorns still range the island as do the deer and some coyotes but only one wild horse remains — an old sorrel — and a mule, the same that Doc used to like to watch buck.

It's unlikely that horses will ever run free again on Wildhorse Island after the deaths of the aging pair.

COWBOYS & COWGIRLS

Champion for six consecutive years at Cheyenne, Tad Lucas has always been admired by rodeo fans. She's considered one of the greatest woman riders in the world. Her first bucking horse contrast was in 1923, in the old Madison Square Garden, in New York. She won second place the first time out. Starting her trick-riding in 1924, she contested at Wimberley, England. Later she won the trick-riding championship at Cheyenne, and held it for several years. She is now the proud owner of the Metro-Goldwyn-Mayer trophy, called at 10 thousand dollars, which was given at Madison Square Garden for the best all-around cowgirl. Surely, Tad Lucas is a "Girl of the Golden West." She is attractive and affectionate in her contacts with those who have worked with and admired her as a girl of the "Range and Rodeo."

Rose Davis was born in Arkansas, but moved to Fort Wroth, Texas, while still a little girl. From her early childhood, her interest was of horses, and as she grew older, she practiced trick-riding. Her real start in the rodeo game came when she signed up to do exhibition riding at a show, and surpassed everyone by coming out on a wild steer. But suffering from a broken leg at Shreveport, Louisiana, she decided to give up the show business. Starting to ride broncs in 1930, she walked out the front gate with plenty of wins. In 1938, she won the cowgirl broncriding championship at Madison Square. But in January 1941, she was killed when alighting from a train. Her husband, Tom Breedon, a top-notch bull-dogger, was killed a year before, when a gun he was handling accidentally went off. It is said that Rose Davis was never thrown, since she started riding in the big shows.

Ella ("Curly") Seale, born at Bell Plains, Texas, could hold her own with most any ranch-hand cowboy at the age of fifteen. A few years ago she was one of the best steer-riders of the world. With her experience gained in riding at such shows as the Fort Worth Rodeo, Oklahoma Roundup, and Texas State Fair Rodeo, Ella represented her hometown at the Stamford County Reunion in 1932. She won the grand prize there. The NF Ranch in Calaban, County, Texas, is owned by Ella Seale.

RED LODGE GREENOUGHS

"Packsaddle" Ben Greenough, wagon-boss of the Montana-Wyoming National Cowboy Association, was born in Illinois, and moved to Brooklyn, New York when just a boy. At the age of seventeen, he went to Montana, where he punched cattle. In 1895, he won the bronc-riding at Billings, in what is said to have been the first rodeo staged in Montana. Ben hadn't left Montana in 53 years, until, in 1939, he went to Madison Square Garden to see his children ride. Ben is the father of Margie, Bill, Alice, and Turk, the four famous Greenoughs. They are great rodeo contestants, real Westerners, and a credit to the game. Alice Greenough and Pete Kerscher were married at Phoenix, Arizona on February 17th, 1940. Alice and Margie can make a lot of fair-riding gents look like amateurs on a horse. Turk Greenough and fan-dancer Sally Rand were married January 6th,

1942, in the Episcopal Church parish hall at Glendora, California. Turk, 36, was divorced from Helen A. Greenough. Sally, 37, listed her real name as Helen Gould Beck. Her father is Wm. F. Beck, a retired army colonel. The Greenoughs will make their home at Heaven Ranch, in Red Lodge, Montana.

MARGIE GREENOUGH, BRONC-RIDER

Margie Greenough is a bronc-rider who wins in many of the famous rodeos throughout the country. She has the stuff, as she showed in Mandan, North Dakota, in 1941. On the third of July, she broke her arm, and on the fourth, there she was riding the tough bronco, "Snow," right into the money. She is married to Heavy Henson, a top steer wrestler, and this fine couple have a boy, nearly ten years old, who stays in Red Lodge while his parents are with rodeos. They don't believe in taking the boy trooping. When six years old, this boy did his first trick roping and riding act in front of a large crowd at a rodeo. He will be a real trooper like those famous parents of his.

ILLUSTRATED STORIES

"CURLY AND JIM" / AKA "The Riders"

We've got two top-ridin' cowhands here on the old Three Cross,
    And both allows he is champion when it comes to ridin' a hoss.
    The other day they were arguin', "Now you listen here!" says Jim,
    "The cowboys have just run in cayuse, an' I don't think you can ride him!"

But Curly, he just laughs an' answers, "Now Jimmy-boy, you just don't know,

"When you're sitting up on an outlaw, you just can't afford to be slow

I've rode 'em all the way down in Texas, I've rode 'em 'way up in Montan!

Well, let's go an' try yer pony, an' if you still think you're best,

An' we can agree on the answer, you're top-ridin' man in the West!"

"Okay, there cowboy," Jim answers, "We'll try the old outlaw now, I'll stay with 'im longer'n you can, an' I'm aimin' to show you just how!

The bronc's a wiry bay mustang, an' Jim he crawls aboard,

He's still tellin' Curly about how he can't be throwed.

A few shakes an' twists from the pony an' Jim he falls off hard,

"I thought you could ride that there pony — you know there were no holts barred!"

Curly, he sure was a-laughin', but Jim glares an' growls up at him,

"You try him, an' by gosh, I betcha your chances will be pretty slim!"

Well, ol' Curly clamps down upon him, and rakes him high and low,

While Jim just stands there watchin', takin in the show.

Finally the ride was all over, and Curly falls off on the ground,

An' now it's Jim's turn for laughin', and he's cup on the hoss with a bound.

The bronc set right into buckin' but Jim stuck him to the last jump,

While Curly sits a-watchin' that bronco was humpin' the hump.

And now it's Jim's turn for bragging, but Curly comes back just as fast,

"You rode him — sure, but remember his worst buckin' spell was past.

I took the kinks, got 'im tired, or you'd never stuck on his back."

"Yeah, but remember he throwed you." Says Curly, "Yeah guess that's a fact.

But look how I piled you the first jump."

"The first jump, my foot!" old Jim cried.

"'Twas a plumb accident that first time, but look at my second ride!"

"Yeah, I saw you ridin' that pony, his head was almost droopin' low,

He was tired from the ride that I gave him." And Jim he swears kinda low.

Now we have rodeos in the cookshack, an' down in the bunkhouse too,

Who'll win the argument finally? Well pardner, that's plumb up to you!

"BESS'S WILD STALLION"

The end of the rope was tangled around the root of a tree

Following the fears and races throughout California in the 1880's, was a Negro they called Bess. He had some fine horses, fast ones that took plenty of prizes. On one of his trips from fear to fair, one of his horses got away during the night and the next day Bess went on without him. He must make the next town in time to race his horses, and he figured to come back to look for the stallion later on.

But the stallion had other plans. He joined a band of wild range horses in the Indian Valley and San Ardo country. These horses were wary and hardened from fleeing the horse runners, and they were all fast too. The slower ones had been caught, and these who couldn't keep up with the tougher bunch, had also been caught, so that now this little band of horses was all of the hardy type, and hard to run down.

They had plenty of speed in the first place, and after the Thoroughbred of Bess's joined them, in a few years there were some speedy half Thoroughbreds running wild on the range. They had the range horse qualities, and also the Thoroughbred speed and life. They were beautiful horses.

There was one especially fine bay stallion to the bunch that cowboys and ranchers had tried to catch for some time. Race horse men offered large rewards for him, and the riders knew if they caught this horse, there was plenty of money in it for them. But the stallion was too smart, and too fast for their horses. They set traps that he successfully eluded, and they ran him for miles, only succeeding in making him wilder and tougher from the miles of running. Many horse fanciers tried to catch him, but without luck. So the stallion "couldn't be taken alive."

One windy day a cowboy called Buck was riding the range when he came upon a bunch of range horses grazing on a grassy slope. He rode toward them, hidden in trees, and with the wind favoring him, and he planned carefully, just how he would catch this fine stallion. For there he was standing hip-shot under a tree, with no idea of a human anywhere in the country. Buck rode as closet s he dared to, and he took down his lariat and kicked his saddle horse into a gallop down the slope and into the open. The wild horses scattered every way, snorting and plunging. The stallion dashed forward as buck and his horse crowded down on him. In his leap for freedom, he forgot to dodge when the lariat spun toward him, and settled over his head. In the second that followed, Buck could see the dollars in his mind that this fine horse would bring — if he could get him to the ranch. But the bay horse hit the end of the rope, and as the saddle horse braced his feet for the jerk, the weight of the captured horse's body snapped the lariat and the wild stallion pitched forward, rolled over and leaped to his feet. He fled like a shot, unhurt, with quite a length of Buck's lariat around his neck, and buck sat his horse with a disappointed look on his face and then broken end of the rope on his saddle horn. He went home with the piece of rope, told his story and said, "No one will ever take him alive."

About a month later a sheep-herder saw a skinny bay stallion standing under a tree. He barely had the strength to stand, and the old man approached him slowly and laid a hand on his neck, where a piece of lariat rope still hung. The other end was fastened tight around a stout street root.

The wild stallion had never been owned by anyone, had never felt a human hand until that day, when this bent and grizzled old man found him under a tree, a broken horse, broken in heart, body, and spirit. There are many old horseman whose eyes get misty as they talk of this grand wild stallion and how he starved to death on the range.

These same old men that say the stallion's blood lives on in the fine horses in California, that there are wild horses that are related to Bess's Thoroughbred that escaped to run wild with the range horses.

"ARABIAN HORSES"

Credit Elsa Jensen

The Arabian — the Horse of the Desert — and the mountains and the hills and the plains, and the show ring. The most beautiful of all horses, and of all horses, the Arab most fully justifies the term "good horse sense." His brain is almost fifty percent larger than that of other horses. The Arabs call him "drinker of air," and their horses are their family.

The Arabian horse is a medium-sized animal, the height at the withers measuring from 14 to 15 hands, with a n occasional horse above or below. Their weight ranges from about 800 to a thousand pounds, with some over or under that weight.

Colonel El Hedad of the Arabian Stud at Babolna, Hungary has this to say about the size of a horse: "We like the small ones every time. In one hundred big horses I find it difficult to select ten good ones. In one hundred small ones, one must look hard to find ten poor ones."

The most common color of Arabians in Arabia, is blood bay, with a black mane and tail, and black legs. These are the most prized. Most Arabians have white markings about the face and legs, but they aren't any pinto Arabians as so many people believe. There are cross-breeds. Some Arabs, however, have sprinklings of rose-colored spots on gray, or are flea-bitten. About thirty percent of the Arabians are bays, fifty percent grays, and fifteen percent chestnuts and browns, with a pure white occasionally, but usually the whites are old horses that once were gray.

Two points of special notice on an Arabian horse are the "mitbah" and the "jibbah." The mitbah is the angle of the neck. The Arabian horse's neck has an angle at the top of the crest that runs to the head, and at the windpipe, running to between the jaws. This gives the horse a beautiful arched neck, and allows for higher carriage of the head and neck, and free movement of the head in all directions. The jibbed is the bulge between the eyes, that runs up to between the ears. This is the very pronounced in colts, and is more prominent in mares than stallions. The jibbed runs down to the nasal bones, which have a "dished" appearance, when viewed from the side.

Something else about the Arabian that one can't miss is the beautifully flashing eyes. They are large and dark brown or black in color, intelligent and gentle, or fiery, depending of course on the horses' feelings. An Arabian stallion prancing with his head high, and proudly lifting his feet, with his big eyes flashing, is indeed a fascinating sight. The eyes are slightly protruding, and enabling the horses to see in all directions, and are shaded by long, thin lashes, as protection from sun, rain and sand. The position of the eyes is more to the center, and to the side, than other breeds of horses.

The Arabian's ears are another point of excellence. They are delicately-made, small and pointed, and are covered with fine, thick hair on the inside, as a protection against desert sand and wind.

The head of the Arab is rather wedge-shaped, wide at the eyes, and with broad jaw-bones, and tapering down to a small muzzle that fits in the palm of a hand. The nostril is long and should lie flat with the face when in repose, and in action, flares wide. The lips are long and thin, and compressed, with the lower lip slightly longer than the upper. Rose-colored noses are often seen in some types of the Arabian.

The windpipe is of unusual size, and hangs loose, which, along with the large nostrils and the deep chest, and strong lungs, allows for freer breathing and accounts for the fact that broken wind or roaring is almost never heard of among the Arabian horses.

The Arabian's neck is so set, and the wind is good enough that these horses can run at top speeds with their necks bowed and their noses on their chests. With the wind-pipe so loose and hanging freely, and the strong lungs, there is another Arabian characteristic that aids in the remarkable strengths of the horse's long-winded strength. This is the broad and deep chest with more space for the area of the lung capacity for taking in more air, the ribs are sprung out wide behind the shoulders and can be plainly seen front or rear, protruding about 2 or 3 inches.

The shoulders are long and set well back, and are firmly and heavily muscled. The withers are high and well set back, and are so heavily muscled they are almost hidden. Arabians are often criticized for not having good withers, by those who do not know this. The good withers and shoulders, as well as the strong forelegs, accounts partly for the weight-carrying and the jumping ability of the Arabian. The front legs seem to have the power to avoid any obstacle in the way, and often an Arabian is seen to strike in the air at a butterfly or at a running dog beside him, with no effort whatsoever.

The back is exceptionally short, as the Arab has 23 instead of 24 vertebrae. This lack of one vertebrae is seldom seen in the crosses. The pelvis is long and nearly level from the croup to the tail. The tail is set at a high point and when the horse is in action, his tail is always carried high and graceful. The quarters are wide and long; the hips and thighs are long and muscular; the hocks are well let down. The croup is slightly higher than the withers. Eclipse, famous race horse was strong in Arabian blood, and he had lower withers than croup. The lowness of the forehand throws more weight in front and increases speed, and in all racing animals the power is needed from behind to propel the animal forward. The greyhound, and the kangaroo are both much lower in front than behind; the popular racing Quarter horses are the same.

The legs of the Arabian are his strongest point. The knees are large, broad and flat; the bone at the back of the knee is very prominent; cannon bone is short, good-sized and very strong. Bones are the weight to be lifted, and it stands to reason that the smallness, the way they occupy less space, and are lighter, as with Arabian horses and deer, would be easier to carry forward than heavy and clumsy legs. The Arabian has the rare strength of power with lightness. The membranes, muscles and sinews are of a lighter, more firm substance. Water on the desert has so much lime, and this partly accounts for the dense bones of the Arabian. The marrow hollow is very small, while the bone around is thicker. The tendons are nearly as large and thick as the cannon bone, and stand out. The past joints are also large and the pastern is neither long enough to be weak, snow short enough to cause a jar when the feet are set down. The feet are small and wide at the heel, round and hard. Splints and win puffs are seldom seen. Any leg ailment, for that matter, is very rare. The Arab's feet are placed lightly and firmly with no jar.

The Arabian's mane and tail grow fine and silky. The tail does not grow so long, as the tail bone has two less vertebrae than other breeds, but the main and foretop grow to a fairly long length as protection from sun, wind and sand. The mane usually lies to the off side. The high, gay tail carriage is a sign of good breeding. There is no need for tail-setting with the Arabian horse.

Arabians develop slowly, and live correspondingly long. Mares reach maturity at about five years, and stallions at a bout six. Mares frequently raise colts up to the age of 25, but, as with stallions, their best years are from five to fifteen. Colts in Arabia are usually broken to ride by the small children, at two or three years, then turned out until they reach five.

Arabians are exceptionally easy-keepers, being used to such foods as the Arabs themselves live on, dates, raw meat, camel's milk, beans, and hay and grain besides. They often go without regular meals, and with two meals in 24 hours, and then only eating handful of beans or some straw and a little barley, and camel's milk, i water is scarce. For colts, the camel's milk is about their only nourishment. They nurse camels freely, and are treated in return as one of the baby camels.

Daumas sums up the Arabian horse as follows: "He should have four points broad, the front, the chest, the croup and the legs; four points long, the neck, the upper parts of the legs, the belly and the hatches; four points short, the loins, the pasterns, the ears, and the tail; The mare ought to take from the wild horse its courage and breadth of head; from the gazelle, the grace, the eyes and mouth; from the antelope, the grace, the liveliness, the intelligence; from the ostrich, its neck and speed; from the viper, the shortness of tail."

The Arab has been trained for the gallop for centuries, and it is his natural gait. The trot is also a good gait, and tests prove that 6 or 7 miles an hour is the best suited for endurance. The Arab's action is long, low, and easy.

It has been proved that the Arabian ranks first among all horses for intelligence. The skull of these horses is wider than three-fourths of its length, and deep from the poll to the eyes, and wide between the eyes, so of course there is more space for brains. Scent is the highest developed sense of the horse. It can recognize its master, follows trails by scent if blindfolded, contaminated feed it will not touch, and poorly ventilated place it will avoid if possible.

The well-used Arabian is a pet. Stallions are gentle as mares, and never altered. However, an Arabian mistreated is almost unequaled for wickedness. And they remember ill treatment, and can recognize and with whoever was responsible, for many years after.

Another outstanding trait of the Arabian is the gentleness and good nature. He is safe for ladies or children to handle, and was picked for unskilled soldiers in the field. Kindness to animals is prates by all the Beduins, though they sometimes let their horses run short of feed —- but not my choice — However, in a case like this, they will go without food, in order to feed their horses. They pet and caress their horses and make pets of the, Instead of whipping or spurring their horses, they treat them with kindness and reason with them, as you would a child. The Arab horse doesn't know cruel treatment and the trust people fully.

The Arabian is the most courageous of all horses. They are often used for hunting lions and tigers, as they will stand up to almost anything.

The Arabs keep records on births, names, colors, markings and breeding of their foals. When a mare is bred, they have witnesses to sign a certificate before a magistrate. A new certificate is signed when the colt is born, with a full description, and date of foaling. These certificates go with the horse if and when he is sold.

As soon as a little colt comes in the desert, it is tied with a string, just about one hock, to a tent stake, and he is left there for the children to play with while his mother goes out to work. It is fed on camel's milk, which the Arabs pretend will give it the camel's strength. At the end of the first month, the colt is weaned. The Bedouins say that unless a colt can do hard work by its third year, it will be almost useless. So during that time he is taken on short trips.

During the winter, the Arabians have no shelter except that of the Arab's tent, and not many horses are able to stand on the sheltered side of a tent at one time. Their hair gets long and shaggy, and they get little feed through the winter too, so they look like half-starved, ragged range ponies. But when spring comes, their beautifully satiny hair brings such change, one would never know them,

Bedouins never use stirrups. They dislike a trot on account of this. They don't use bit in a horse's mouth, only a halter with a chain over the nose.

There are five strains of Arabians: Kehilan (Kuhaylan), Seglawi (Saq-lawi), Abeyan, Hamdani, and Hadban.

Kehilan: The most numerous, and generally, the most esteemed. More bays than other strains. Fasted, through not the hardiest. Substrains are Kehilan Ajuz, Kehilan Nowag, Kehilan Abu Argub, Abu Jenub, and Ras-el-Fedawi.

Seglawi: One strain, Seglawi-Jedran, considered best in the desert, held in high repute. A rare strain. Other strains, Obeyran, Arjebi, and el-Abd, but only Selawi-Jerdan is pure.

Abeyan: Called the handsomest breed, smaller than others; substrings, Abeyan Sherrak.

Hamdani: Most of this breed are grays. Substrain, Hamdani Simri. A beautiful strain, with longer ears, an uncommon breed.

Hadban: Alos uncommon; substrains, Mshetib and El Furrd, and Enzekhi. There are 16 other breeds besides these five, though not popular ones.

The Arabian is the most common ancestor of all our superior light horses, the Morgan, Thoroughbred, American Saddler, and the Western ponies also. In Europe, Arabian blood was used to improve the war horses, and also the work stock. The Percheron horse's best qualities are traceable to the Arabian.

For their size, the Arabian horse has no superior in weight carrying. He is said to have the manners of a gentleman, and the gentle disposition of a well-bred woman.

Almost alone out of 27 horses, a purebred Arab gelding from the Crabbett Stud in England, came through in an endurance race of 310 miles over concrete and macadam roads, to win first. He carried 245 pounds, and covered the distance at a trot, and suffered no bad after affects, no sore feet or pindpuffs, or strained tendons.

Arabians are excellent jumpers, One mare, when she arrived from England, easily cleared a fence five feet six inches high, More than ninety-five percent of the winners of the Classic English Races (Derby, Oaks, and St. Legger,) are descendants of the Arab. This is from the beginning of the racing. Native Arabs, with the Barbs, are the source of our race horses of today.

George Washington's famous gray horse, Nelson, was a son of the desert-born Arabian, Ranger, imported to New London, Connecticut, in about 1765. He was fifteen hands, a dapple gray, and of the finest form. Washington was 6 feet 3 inches and weighed over 200 pounds, so the little gray horse Nelson, must have been a weight carrier.

To known an Arabian is to love an Arabian. The most beautiful, the strongest for his size, the friendliest, the hardest of all horses. The only thing an Arabian can honestly be compared to, in beauty, grace, speed, strength and style, is the deer.

FAY'S POETRY

"The Song of a True American"

From the far North to the Southland, from the East to the West,
    We will keep Old Glory waving o'er the land that we love best;
We will stand behind our soldiers, on the land and on the sea,
    And we're proud to do our best to help keep America free.

In the land, on air, on water, the U S A shall reign,
    Through the sweat and toil and sorrow, through the tears and through the pain;
We shall fight for home and freedom, fight with everything we can,
    Back our soldiers to the limit — we will stand by every man!

"Cowboy's Farewell"

Take my boots an' chaps an' saddle
    And hang 'em on the wall,
Turn my horse out on the prairie,
    Until some other fall.

Take my good ol' Western outfit
    When I join the soldiers brave,
In my U.S. soldier's outfit-
    This land I'm out to save!

So adios, old pardners,
    I'll be comin' back some day,
When we've licked those sons of Satan,
    And this land is free to stay!

"Mist O'er the Valley"

There's a mist across the valley
   And the mountains to the west,
The sun is slowly sinking,
   The birds have gone to rest.

I gaze out toward the westland
   Thinking of my cowboy true,
Who is helping Uncle Sam
   And our own red, white, and blue.

A sad and lonely pony,
   Stands with dark head hanging low,
It's been so long since this cowboy,
   Rode his pony, Little Joe.

Sad dark eyes turn to the west hills,
   Where his master last was seen,
Then back to me — he's pleading
   To bring him back again.

Chaps and spurs and saddle
   Are hanging on the wall,
And no more in the evening,
   Will we hear our cowboy's call

Till our land is free from danger
   And we're free to roam the hills,
As the mist comes o'er the valley
   And we hear the whip-por-wills.

GRACE LARSON

"Sunset in the West"

There's a land that's full of beauty
    And you'll like it better yet
When you see the range turn golden
    As the sun begins to set.
Your city lights are wonders,
    But here's what I love best:
To see the golden splendor
    Of the sunset in the west.

The sagebrush turns to silver
    As the moon comes shining through,
When the golden sun is setting —
    That's a scene of beauty too.
Come out to our Westland,
    There are times you won't forget
When the range is gold and lovely,
    And the sun begins to set.

"God Bless Our Soldier Boys"

Our soldier boys are marching,
    They've heard their country's call,
From East to West, from North to South,
    They've come to give their all;
God bless our soldier boys,
    Who have answered to our call,
Gallantly they march away,
    To join their comrades all.

In the ever-growing forces
    Of the air and the land and the sea,
In answer to their Nation's need,
    In defense of liberty.
God bless our soldier boys,

So brave and strong and true,
  Marching on to victory,
    'Neath the old Red, White, and Blue;
For home and for liberty,
  For allegiance to our flag, they stand,
God bless our soldier boys,
  Who defend this mighty land!

"Turnabout"

Hitler an' Mussolini were talkin' on one day,
  Said Herr Hitler to his neighbor, "We got der hell to pay!
We were tryin' to get der Russians, but hey it's mighty strong,
  Do you think dat you can help us — oh, it wont be very long —"

"Very long till what, Herr Hitler? You mean till you are gone?"
  Der Fuehrer roared, "You dummy! Till der rest of dem is gone
If you help then I'll help you, in any time of need.
  Ain't dot fair" Says Mussolini, "Yes, it's very fair indeed!
"When you've gone and licked the Russians, which I'm sure you'll never do,
Then you'll turn and try to get us — that's just what I know — do you?
But you will never get us 'cause you've got both hands full,
  When you say that you will help us, that is just a lot of bull!

"I know just what you are now, the worst that I have seen
  You would rob your helpless neighbors, you would steal your own folks clean!"

"But, dear friend, if you would help me, why I'll tell you what I'll do,
  First I'll lick the Russian army, then (I might start in on you)
I will take the other countries, and I'll put them all in one,
Make a brand new German country — now wouldn't that be fun?"

'Twould be fun for you, dear Hitler, but what about the rest?
  We'd all pile up on you, while you feathered your old nest.
We would beat you to a frazzle, and you'd sure look a fright,
  You'd help me like I'd help you - you'd help me all right!"

GRACE LARSON

"FAY'S LAST POEMS: #1"

In the pages of history are written
This story of two men brave and true
Two heroes who fought for their country,
As only two heroes can do.

They fought till the World War was over,
For their homes and the freedom of men.

For they helped bring the war to an end.

"FAY'S LAST POEMS: #2"

And the thought never came for a moment
That this was to be their last fight,
And then oer the waves flashed a message,
How our brave heroes were not in sight,

And a great vessel went fourth to the rescue,
For they knew that the ship went down

There's a lesson to learn from this story,
How our life is a ship on its way
We all should be ready
When the Master calls us someday.

"Snowbound Cowboy"

It is snowin' on the prairie,
    An' the wind is howlin' wild,
A cowboy's huntin' dogies,
    An' his cussin' sure ain't mild,
For there's snow on his new saddle,
    And in his collar too,
He's caught miles from the home-ranch,
    On his tired pony, Blue.

He cusses Mother Nature
    For bringin' on a storm,
When it's least expected,
    An' most likely to do harm,
For the cows ain't quite all rounded,
    An' there's some ponies too,
That should be fed this winter,
    To find 'em's hard to do.

But when you've rode the ranges
    Like this cussin' buckaroo,
You take the snow or sunshine,
    Without so much to-do,
He's learned to weather hardships,
    'Cause when his work is done,
He makes up for it on pay-day,
    In town a-havin' fun.

"The Moon is Swingin' High"

Oh, the moon was swingin' high
    In a starry summer sky,
    As we whispered a tender last adieu,
You said "Sweetheart, adios,"
And you held me up so close,

Then you whispered, "Darlin', sweet, how I love you."
I'm so lonely, sad, and blue,
Just a-waiting, dear, for you,
We will meet again 'neath skies of midnight blue,
When the moon is swingin' high in a starry summer sky,
   I'll be waitin', dear, a-waitin' just for you.

"I'm Waiting for You"

For years I have waited for you, dear,
   Hoping you'd come back to me,
But this is waiting has all been in vain, dear,
   And I guess it just couldn't be.

CHORUS:
   When the leaves are all turning yellow,
      And the white frost is on the ground,
   Remember our days together,
      And the happiness that we found.
You left me and went with another
   When you knew that I loved you true,
You care not if my heart is broken,
   But I am still waiting for you.

REPEATE CHORUS:
I'll always keep right on waiting,
   And someday you might return
Remember, my dear, I still love you,
   And for you the flame in my heart burns.

"In the Heart of Montana"

Way up in the heart of Montana,
   Where a sad-hearted girl waits for you,
The days are so endless with longing
   For this cowgirl who loves you so true.

These pleading words I hear her saying:
    "Oh cowboy, come back to your love
Who waits in the Heart of Montana,
    'Neath the stars that shine from above.

"You left me alone in the Springtime,
    And drifted along one sad day,
Left a cowgirl to mourn for her lover,
    Just pining her life all away.

"Remember that day you left me,
    The skies of Springtime were blue,
You told me that you'd be returning,
    And always your heart would be true."

She waits in the Heart of Montana,
    And the skies have all turned to gray,
Oh, cowboy, come back to your love,
    Before Heaven takes her away.

"Our Paradise"

Shadows creep over the valley,
    Twilight is falling around,
Coyotes howl in the moonlight,
    Hear their sad mournful sound.
When the moon shines over the valley,
    On the sagebrush and mesquite,
It's silvery beams kills the hill-tops,
    And make our heaven complete.

Just a little ranch here in the valley,
    With the only one I love,
The beautiful hills all surround us,
    The moon's peeping down from above.
Cares float away with the breezes,

Here in our paradise,
We're ridin' this old trail homeward.
As the moon sails through the sky.

"Lonely Cowboy"

The moon shines over the tree-tops,
    The clouds are floating on high,
Tiny stars blink in the heavens,
    The breezes gently blow by,
I'm longing for you and the rangeland,
    Where long ago I used to roam,
Oh why did I ever leave you?
    I'm lonely and wish I was home.

I wonder if you are still waiting,
    For the cowboy you promised to love?
I miss you so much, and I'm lonely,
    As the pale moon shines down from above.
Memories keep lingering with me,
    I know that I'll soon hit the trail,
Back to my rangeland and you, dear,
    Down there in that green shady dale.

"It's a Long, Lonesome Trail"

-published in 1st June, '42 *Ranch Romances*.

It's a long, lonesome trail when you travel alone,
    Darling, I wish you were here,
The days when we were together, my love,
    To my memory are so clear.
The trail seems so long without you, my own,
    For you've found another you love,
Now my old pinto pony travels along,
    And I gaze at the heavens above.

Down this long, lonesome trail my pony jogs on,
    I'm lonely, and wish you were here,
I remember this trail in the days long gone by,
    When you rode with me, dear.
Move along, my little old pinto pal,
    I know you never will fail,
Someday my darling may call me back,
    Until then, we'll stay on the trail.

"When the Golden Sun Goes Down"

When the golden sun goes down,
    I'm gonna hit the trail for home,
I'm so tired of travelin' 'round,
    Wish I'd never come to roam.

There's a girl a-waitin' there,
    An' I know that she'll be true,
It's more than I can bear,
    Just a-longin', dear, for you.

Soon I'll see the old home ranch,
    And the range once more I'll ride,
Down where the old trails branch,
    With my darling by my side.

When the golden sun goes down,
    I'll be back there on the range,
I'm so tired of roamin' 'round,
An' I'm longin' for a change.

"Lonesome"

The sky is so gray and cloudy,
    And the moon is sailing high,
A disk so cold and dreary,
    Not like in days gone by.

There's are tears in my eyes, darling,
    And my heart's feeling sore,
You left me broken-hearted,
    And I'll see you no more.

Once when the moon was shining,
    My heart from cares was free
You said you would love me forever,
    But now what will happen to me?

There are tears in my eyes, darling,
    And deep in my heart there's a sigh,
Oh why did you ever leave me,
    Alone in the dusk to cry?

"Why Did You Leave Me?"

Why did you leave me,
    When always you knew,
How much I love you,
    And how I was true?

Why did you kiss me,
    And then turn away,
And leave me alone
    On that sad, dreary day?

No reason you gave me,
    Just, "Thank you, my dear

For all of the pleasures,
    And days filled with cheer.

"Forgive me, my darling,
    And don't you forget
That I've always loved you,
    And still love you yet."

"Goodbye." And you left me,
    Oh why did you go,
And leave me alone,
    When you love me, I know?

"In Old Mexico"

The sky is my blanket
    And under my head
My saddle's my pillow,
    The ground is my bed.

Memories linger
    From long, long ago,
Taking me back there
    To Old Mexico.

Oh, do I not hear her —
    That voice soft and low-
The girl I once knew
    Down in Old Mexico?

That smile, that sweet laughter,
    Her voice soft and low,
Is only an echo
    From days long ago.

Her memory haunts me -

Oh why did I go
And leave her alone
   Down in Old Mexico?

"Bronc-Rider's Song to His Cowgirl"

You're brave and game and a beauty,
   My sweet, untainted wild rose,
You're always right there a-yelling
   For me at the big rodeos.
You can ride and rope with the cowboys,
   My dear little rodeo queen,
With your sparkling brown eyes, and your sweet smile,
   Grandest girl that I've ever seen.

The rodeo gets in your blood, dear,
   The cowboys and horses, you know,
The wild broncos stamping around you,
   You see why I love the big show.
But this is no life for you, cowgirl,
   It's hard and it's dangerous too,
Just stay on the ranch in the mountains,
   And maybe I'll come there to you.

But someday from one of the big shows,
   Your cowboy may never return,
Don't shed any tears for me, darling,
   Although your poor heart will yearn.
For it's all in the life of a cowboy,
   Just like any other tough game —
I've always loved those wild horses,
   And I'll always love them the same.

A bronc-rider's life is uncertain
   He's only here for today,
And tomorrow a wild bronc stamps on him,

And carries his soul away.
Then please don't cry for me, darling,
    For I'm not worth it to you,
But you're a sweet kid an' I love you,
    'Cause you're a bronc-bustin' gal too.

"Answer to 'It's All Over Now"

You say that it's all over now, dear,
    That your waiting has all been in vain,
But today, little girl, I'm returning,
    For the rest of my days to remain.

It's never too late, you have told me,
    And your love for me always holds true,
You were right, dear, because I still love you,
    And I soon will be back there with you.

Your prayers are now answered, my darling,
    And my heart will forever be true,
I know I was wrong when I left, dear,
    But now I'm returning to you.

"Love's Rodeo"

I'm entered in Love's Rodeo,
    I'm training for the prize
That's hidden in your golden hair,
    And lurks within your eyes.

I'm entered in Love's Rodeo,
    I'm training for the chance
To loop my rope around your heart,
    And round up **true** romance.

"Sweetheart"

I thought that you would like to know
    That someone's thoughts go where you go,
That someone never can forget
    The hours we spent since first we met;
That life is richer, sweeter, far,
    For such a sweetheart as you are;
And now my constant prayer will be,
    That God will keep you safe for me.

"Western Gal"

She's a Western girl with a Western way,
    This little cowgirl of mine,
She's a wild, sweet rose of the prairie,
    And you bet your life she's fine.
You can talk of Lana or Hedy or Ann,
    But with her they'll never compare —
She's a beauty, as sweet as a flower,
    As pure as the prairie air.

I've seen her ride over the prairies,
    As straight and as proud as a queen,
No lovelier picture has ever been known,
    And still remains to be seen.
She named the day for our wedding to be,
    When over the hills we did ride,
Then that Western girl with the Western way
    Will be my little cowgirl bride!

"Longing for You"

I wonder as I ride down the trail tonight,
    Why do the stars fail to shine,
Why does the moon seem so pale tonight,
    Since you are no longer mine?

Dark clouds fill the sky, as I'm ridin' by,
    They hide the moon's silvery beams,
I never thought it would be this way
    That you'd be mine only in dreams.

"There'll be a Blue Sky"

There'll be a blue sky on the morrow
    When the dark clouds roll away,
There'll be sunshine and happiness
    And our cares will float away,
We'll be happy as the world rolls along,
    And we'll all be a-singin' a song,
There'll be a blue sky on the morrow,
    And we'll sing our cares away.

"Pride and a Broken Heart"

We've said goodbye, but I didn't cry,
    Although my heart has turned to stone,
Memories won't let my poor heart forget,
    But you'll soon forget that I'm alone.
Friends I shall meet when walking the street,
    But never will they hear me sigh;
Pride will help me hide the broken heart inside,
    And since we've parted, none will ever see me cry.

"Kentucky and You"

My heart's pining for old Kentucky,
    I'm always lonely and blue,
Wish I was back in Kentucky,
    There in the wildwood with you.
We parted in anger but I still love you, dear,
    In dreams I'm with you and it's more than I can bear;
Now I'm drifting back to my homeland,
    To Kentucky and you.

"A Dream"

Last night I dreamed that I saw you,
    My smile was bright and sure,
And you never guessed how uncertain
    My heart and footsteps were.
Your eyes searched mine just an instant
    To find some remaining trace
Of the love and devotion I once had,
    Showing upon my face.

You thought then that I had forgotten,
    That years hid all the pain,
And I thought I could smile, dear,
    If we should meet again
But today I really did see you,
    My love was plain to see,
And now I just couldn't help thinking —
    How wrong a dream can be!

"June Night"

Sometimes I regret the time that we met,
    That quiet, happy evening in June,
I thought that night my heart had chosen right,
    When it started singing love's old Tune.
But you play with my love like it meant nothing to you,
    I'd beg for your love, but what good would it do?
Maybe you'd learn, if we could but return
    To that starry June-night long ago,
To give me your heart, but it's best we should part,
    Although it means heartbreak, I know.

"Lover's Lane"

Wandering alone, I found my sweetheart,

Down in Lover's Lane;
I longed for companionship, someone to love,
    Someone to still my heart's pain.
She stood alone, her eyes filled with tears,
    I held her close to my heart.
We knew that day down in Lover's Lane,
    Our love was meant from the start.

"A Dream of Long Ago"

I used to know, long, long ago,
    That you loved me true;
I used to see when you'd look at me,
    Love, in your dear eyes of blue.
But now I find in my weary mind,
    Memories are paining me so,
I used to know that you loved me so,
    But now that's a dream of long ago.

"Sagebrush in the Spring"

by Grace Larson

Just a glance out toward the Westland
 To your heart a thrill will bring,
When the moon shines o'er the valley,
 On the sagebrush in the Spring.

The stars are shining brightly
 And the moon is riding high,
The sage is gently rustling
 From a breeze a-blowing by.

Just listen to the night-birds,
 Hear their wild calls ring,
When the moon is drawing pictures
 On the sagebrush in the Spring.

"Gee, I Wish I Had a Horse!"

(4/20/67)

Gee, I wish I had a horse to ride on day by day.
Anything would do, of course, a chestnut or a bay;
A pinto sure would fill the hill, or maybe just a black,
And if I got a plain old gray I wouldn't send it back!

A little pony, cute and tame with great big dark brown eyes,
Or else a tall, majestic horse that runs so fast it flies;
A wild mustang with tangled mane, defiance in his eyes.
I wouldn't mind a runaway, or even one that shies.

A small one or a tall one, any color, shape or size
Would fill my heart with gladness, and be a great surprise.
I'd care for it and feed it and brush it every day,
I'd never ask for anything, except perhaps some hay!

If I could only have my wish, a pony for a pal,
A horse that I could call my own to keep in my corral.
Gee, I wish I had a horse like other people do!
The only way I'd change my wish, would be to wish for two!

"Lost Pal"

There's a tired and heartsick cowgirl gazing off across the range,
The old corral is empty and she's feeling mighty strange;
Her faithful old cowpony is a-missing from his stall,
And this poor cowgirl is lonely for the truest pal of all.

For many years they rode the range in sunshine and in rain, —
This little old cowpony with the long and silvery mane.
But now she's left for the rangeland, and this cowgirl's heart is sore,
And she's crying for this little horse that she'll see nevermore.

"There'll be a Green Pasture"

There'll be a green pasture for you, old pal,
    Up on that heavenly range,
You'll be lonely, I know, as you're grazing,
    In a pasture that's new and strange.
But I will soon join you up there, old pal,
    For my last race is just about run,
And we'll travel along, while I sing a cowboy song,
    When our roundup on earth is done.
We'll meet all our old pals up yonder,
    We'll rope and we'll brand as in the days of yore,
When we head for that scene where the hills are all green,
    'Way up on that heavenly range.

"Blue Sky"

There'll be a blue sky on the morrow,
    When the dark clouds roll away,
There'll be sunshine and happiness,
    And our cares will float away,
We'll be happy as the world rolls along,
    And we'll all be a-singin' a song;
There'll be a blue sky on the morrow,
    And we'll sing our cares away.

"Mary of the Prairie"

There's a girl in this here town,
    An' at ridin' she's the best,
She just came ridin' down,
    She's the Girl of the Golden West.

CHORUS:
    If you see a gal that don't give a heck,
    A-ridin' like she's tryin' to bust her neck,

        That's Mary of the Prairie, Pride of the Rodeo.
All she does is ride out after cattle,
On a good top-horse and a fancy flowered saddle,
If you see a gal that's pretty as a peach,
Stickin' to a bucker just like a leech,
        That's Mary of the Prairie, Pride of the Rodeo.

"Alone"

So lonely and wear an old cow horse
    Is standing alone on the hill,
His days are numbered and dim are his eyes,
    This little cowpony, Bill.
It's been years since he went on the roundups,
    It's been ages since he tasted hay,
Now he's left alone on the lonely prairie,
    Cold and starving today

God pity and care for this little cowhorse,
    He's done his job faithfully,
Take care of him there on that heavenly range,
    Where no pain or sorrow he'll see.
He's so tired and weary and he doesn't care,
As he stands there alone on the hill,
He knows he'll soon head for the range in the sky,
    This little ol' cowpony, Bill.

"Hosses"

Now horses they ain't just machines
    You run across the ground,
They're the best pals and companions,
    That I have ever found;
Take that old bay there, for instance,
    See that scar upon his side?
The Indians darn near got us,
    I thought it was our last ride.

He outran 'em an' took me to safety,
    Seemed worried for fear I was hurt,
Why never in all of his ridin'
    Has he felt a spur or quirt.
When you see a worn-out cayuse
    Like that brown pony standin' there,
Don't laugh 'cause he looks scrubby,
    An' has rough an' shaggy hair.

If you laugh you just don't know hosses,
    Just ask any ol' cowhand.
An' he'll tell you that little bronco
    Was once the best in the land.
Them ol' cowhosses are favorites,
    As pals and companions too,
They'll seldom refuse to obey you,
    And they'll always take you through.

On a cold and frost mornin'
    When you sling the saddle on,
That gray there starts to buckin'
    But he's just havin' some fun.
Lots of broncs do the same thing,
    When they're tryin' to keep warm,
He ain't really tryin' to hurt you,
    An' he sure don't mean no harm.

See that little ol' Palomino,
    With her fine head hangin' low,
An' that little colt there beside her—
    Once she sure was far from slow.
Could head off the fastest critter
    That ever grew a horn —
The toughest little pony
    That ever has been born.

When you start pokin' fun at
    The little ones whose ribs all show,
Like, this paint pony nuzzlin' at me —
    Now much of hosses you know.
For these broncs are just like a person,
    An' they should be treated fine,
For you bet they sure deserve it,
    Every nine time out of nine!!!

"Don't Believe It"

Pay no attention to the rider
    Who says he's never fell
From off a buckin' bronco,
    He's just talkin', you know well.

As a kid when he was tryin'
    To ride a buckin' hoss,
There's many times the ponies
    Showed the younker who was boss.

"Though it's nothin' they take pride in,
    Every cowboy that I've knowed,
If he's ever done much ridin',
    He's at different times been throwed."

No truer words were spoken,
    An' I would swear to that,
An' the guy who says he can't be throwed
    Is talkin' through his hat!

GRACE LARSON

"Wet Stirrups" (March 17, '43)

When the rain has been a-fallin',
    An' your saddles gettin' wet,
You're soaked from head to foot,
    An' you're feelin' bad, you bet,
You climb down from your pony,
    To open up a gate,
When you turn back to the Cayuse,
    He don't want so much to wait.

As you start to crawl aboard him,
    He snorts an' starts to shy,
But you swing into the saddle
    An' your pony hits the sky.
You forgot how it's been rainin',
    As you mount him with a bound,
Your foot slips from the stirrup,
    An' you're throwed upon the ground.

You're sittin' in a mud-hole,
    You cuss him for no brains,
You know you got some walkin',
    For he's halfway 'cross the plains.
When you step into the saddle
    On a cold an' rainy day,
Jab your boots deep in the stirrups,
    For you want 'em there to stay!

"I'll Meet You at the Roundup in the Spring"

Old pal, you're getting tired, and you can work no more,
    You're heading for a good long rest upon that other shore.
Where you'll have all the pleasures that life could ever bring,
    Now goodbye, old pal, I'll meet you at the roundup in the spring.

Oh, I'll meet you at the roundup in the Spring, old pal,
    Upon that happy range where all friends go,
We'll ride this land no more, but there we'll have everything,
    So farewell, ol' boy, I'll meet you at the roundup in the Spring.

"Farewell, Buckaroo"

You're leaving the range when you've ridden
    In sunshine, snow, and in rain,
You're leaving the cattle and ponies,
    And cowboys with hearts filled with pain.

The Big Boss has ordered a roundup,
    He needed someone to ride guard
And watch o'er the strays 'way up yonder,
    Where herding will not be so hard.

Farewell, buckaroo, we'll miss you,
    And think of you lots as we ride,
Our hearts will be with you, old pardner,
    While you're riding herd 'cross the Divide.

"The Pal That I Knew Long Ago"

Written in memory of Pal's mother, Belle, who died July 17th, 1940, at the age of fourteen years.

In a vine-shaded grave in the valley,
    Where the meadow-lark flies to and fro,
Near a stream that flows down from the mountains,
    Lies a pal that I knew long ago.

Just a little gray pony, my pardner,
    For years we rode down the long trail,
How I miss her when shadows are creeping,

'Round my little old home in the dale.

There were times we were happy together,
    Rode the ranges and roundup of strays,
And deep down inside, my poor heart aches,
    For my pal of roundup days.

Seems that I hear a call from the meadow,
    The call that she gave, soft and low,
But it's only a memory that lingers
    Of the pal that I knew long ago.

"Monarch of the Plain"

He stands there defiant,
    Against the blue sky,
Monarch of the Prairie,
    With head and tail high.

His small band of ponies
    Are waiting below,
For their leader's message
    Which tells them to go.

A beautiful mustang
    With long, tangled mane,
May he always rule
    As Monarch of the Plain.

"Old Pardners"

There's a tired and weary cowboy
    Fazing off across the plain,
His roundup days are over,
    And he'll never ride again.

An old and faithful pony
    Stands with head turned to the West,
He recalls those days of riding
    With the pal he loves the best.

The cowboy gazes at him,
    Wipes a tear-drop from his eye,
And he says, "Well, pard, we'll soon be
    Herdin' doggies in the sky.

"Ol' boy, we're gettin' tired,
    At the end of our life's trail,
But no sir, I won't worry,
    'Cause I know you'll never fail.
"I recall those good ol' days,
    When we always used to ride,
And you'd trot down the valley —
    We were always satisfied.

"Ol' boy, we'll find a new range,
    An' it won't be very long,
'Cause we're driftin' on to Heaven,
    Where our life will be a song.

"I can see you there a-grazin',
    I can hear your old call ring,
As it echoes o'er the valley,
    Through the sage-brush in the spring."

"There's a Rainbow 'Cross the Hills of Ol' Montana"

There's a rainbow 'cross the hills of old Montana,
    And the clouds are slowly drifting from the sky,
There's a mist across the river in the valley,
    And the nightingale is slowly soaring by;
The sun will soon be gone, but I'll keep travelin' on,

There's a rainbow 'cross the hills of old Montana,
    And it calls me to that Western home of mine.

"There's a Heaven A-Waitin'"

There's a heaven a-waitin' for you, old pal,
    Up there on that heavenly shore,
Where you will find rest in that land farther west,
    And you'll never work anymore.
You've done your job faithfully and without fail
    Old pal, you've been truer than gold.
There's a heaven a-waitin' down the last trail,
    In the land where you'll never grow old.

"Barrel Racer"

We rounded the first one and flew for the second,
Then off for the third barrel, just perfection, I reckon.
And back to the finish line… crowd on its feet,
Just made a run that couldn't be beat.
Raked all my winnings in a big silver cup,
Alarm clock jangled… then I woke up!

"That Beat-Up Ol' Brown Hat"

She rode her horses everywhere, in rain or sun or snow;
She headed for the mountains on that morning long ago.
"Hey, wait a bit!" I wonder what she's going back to find,
And out she comes, "I plumb forgot that ol' brown hat of mine,"

She used to ride and do it well, and does a little yet,
But this is now and that was then, and there's one thing I'll bet,
Her souvenirs and memories would be something to behold.
As she looks back in fondness on those happy days of old.

Many things forgotten and lost along the line,

Cast aside and covered by the drifting sands of time.
But things she'll never part with, and you can bet on that,
Her faithful saddle horses and that beat-up ol' brown hat!

"Sunset"

I never knew what it was to be blue,
    'Til you went away last night.
We'd only met a few hours before,
    But our love just seemed to be right.

You left at the coming of sunset,
    Not knowing when you would return,
It's sunset again 'cross the valley,
    And my heart in sadness does yearn.

"Pal"

A pal is more than just a friend,
    For friends may come and go,
But on a pal you can depend
    To stick right by, you know,
And that is why you're "Pal" to me —
    Because I know so well
How loyal you will always be,
    And 'cause I know you're swell!

"Spring on the Range"

When the moon shines on the sagebrush,
    And the stars on high wheel free,
Then I feel the West is calling,
    And that's where I long to be.

When the cattle on the rangeland
    Crop the grass that's growing there,

Then I feel the West is calling,
    And it's more than I can bear.
For there's moonlight on the canyon,
    And there sounds the coyote's wail,
And it's Spring out on the mesa,
    And I long to hit the trail.

For I miss the cattle bawling,
    Long to hear the nightbirds sing,
To see the splendor of the moonlight,
    On the sagebrush in the Spring.

"To a Cowboy"

From out earth's dusty old corral,
    When failures press,
May every bronco that you rope
    Be named "Success."
May winter's Northers spare thy range,
    And pass thee o'er,
And blizzards never pile snow-drifts
    At thy door
And as you follow life's long trail,
    Round cliff and bend,
May strangers make the Indian sign
    That means "A friend."
And at evening time
    May it come to pass
You find yourself on Peaceful Creek,
    And on good grass,
And when the final roundup comes,
    Some Autumn day,
May your brand in the Book of Life
    Be this: "O.K."

"Cowpoke's Vacation"

The other night the boss told us,
    "Wal, boys, you can all head for town.
You've worked pretty hard on the roundup,
    This week-end, you'd best lay around.
"Draw your pay, get your Sunday duds on,
    Saddle up that slick-curried hoss,
You'll find all your gals are a-waitin',
    An' maybe some friends run across."

I slicked up a-tryin' to look purty,
    To all of them cowgirls' eyes,
Put on a silk shirt an' my best pants,
    An' saddled my old bronc, Blue Skies.

I drawed my wages, says "So long,"
    An' off with the boys I did go,
I gives a wild yip an' a holler,
    "Come on bronc, you're goin' too slow!"

When I hit town I left Blue Skies,
    A-munchin' his oats in the barn,
Then I heads for the bar and red likker,
    From then on, I don't give a darn.

I sets 'em up for the cowboys,
    An' after I drink a few down,
I feel like I'm light as a feather,
    An' the room goes whirlin' around.

I reach out to steady the walls,
    'Cause they look sorta shaky to me,
I reach for a chair as it goes by,
    But it goes too darn fast, you can see.

Then I took a swipe at the bar,
    'Cause it sure was gonna take a spill,
When I woke I was half-drowned in a horse-trough,
    Guess the fellers thought I'd had my fill.

So I headed back for the old ranch,
    'An back to a-herdin' them cattle,
'Til next pay-day, that's just where I'll stay,
    A-livin' all day in my saddle.

"Cow Pasture on the Moon"

This Great Society will build new life for all concerned,
And give us lives of good and ease with no expenses spurned.
They take away, then give it back in gestures oh, so grand!
They tell us what to raise, and how, they even take our land.

Railroads, highways, dams and parks are taking all the grass,
And fences cut across the range, and buggies run on gas.
And grain fields wave where one time only cows and ponies grazed,
And buffalo and deer and elk and antelopes were raised.

To do an honest, full-day's work is "fourteen-ninety-two,"
With coffee-breaks and over-time compensation too.
Years ago the cowboy's day was dawn 'till after dark;
He helped to build this land of ours, 'twas there he left his mark.

These modern days have brought a big change to the cowboy's ways,
Not many places do they live as in the olden days.
With sad heart now he views the range where once he used to ride;
He sees a city growing here with no highways on each side.

And through the center of the once-free range he used to know,
He sees a dam back up a lake where cattle used to grow.
Each year the range gets smaller, so we must find out soon:
With all the treasures, will they find cow pasture on the moon?

He's backed up to the mountain tops where naught but grass will grow,
But pretty soon they'll find a way to build up there, you know.

He looks concerned and wonders how and where we'll raise our cows,
In the future days of crowding, it ain't easy he allows!

With Uncle Sam a-shootin' all those billions in the air,
Trying for soft landings and to see what all's up there.
But what concerns the cowboy is: (He hopes they'll find out soon)
Among those treasures, could there be cow pasture on the moon?

"To a Cowboy"

In the old corral of life
    When things go wrong,
May skies be blue and cloudless,
    Around you, a song;
May storms and hardships pass you,
    And bring you no harm,
And in winter, a cheery fire
    To keep you warm;
And when you ride on Westward,
    May your journey be free
From cares, hardships, and sorrows,
    New pastures you'll see.
May old cowboy pals meet you
    In that new land,
And your new Boss greet you,
    And shake your hand.
Your faithful cowpony call you
    Far from hillside,
And 'round the doggies in heaven,
    You're free to ride.

GRACE LARSON

"Farewell, Buckaroo"

You're leaving the range where you've ridden
    In sunshine, snow, and in rain,
You're leaving the cattle and ponies,
    And cowboys, with hearts filled with pain.

The Big Boss has ordered a roundup,
    He needs someone to ride guard,
And watch o'er the strays 'way up yonder,
    Where herding will not be so hard.

Farewell, buckaroo, we'll sure miss you,
    And think of you lots as we ride,
Our hearts will be with you, old pardner,
    While you're riding herd 'cross the Divide.

FAY'S PENCIL ART

Fay's art work

He'd set back and snort —

We pulled him for 3 hours, uphill and downhill.

Redskin..... boy, he was some hoss!

The end of the rope was tangled around the root of a tree

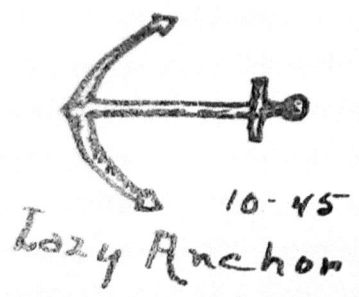

Lazy Anchor 10-45

A sleepy-looking horse, that old "Buckskin" — but what a surprise when you got on him — sometimes...

FAY'S OIL PAINTINGS

"MY MOTHER, ANNIE MAE DESCHAMPS"

UNPUBLISHED POETRY:

FOR YOU
 by Mae Poloson

I believe that God above
Created you for me to love,
He picked you out from all the rest
Because He knew who I loved best.

I once had a heart it's true
But now it's yours, from me to you.
Take good care of it, as I have none.

If I go to Heaven and you are not there
I'll paint your name on the golden stair
So all the angels know & see
Just what you really mean to me.

If you are not there by judgment day,
I'll know you have gone the other way.
I will give the angels back their wings
And golden harps and everything.

Then just to show you what I'd do
I'd go down below to be with you.

IT'S JUST A MATTER OF TIME

It's just a matter of time 'till the bombs start to fall
And all the rats in Tokyo will start to squeal and ball,
We won't forget to say 'so sorry, 'scuse me'
Then we'll kick their honorable seat of the pants clear to their honorable knees.

A lesson they're gonna learn when we start getting rough
When Sherman said the war was hell,
He didn't say half enough
They're gonna regret the day they stabbed us in the back
'Cause somethings going to fall
When the Yankees start to smack.

It's just a matter of time till we'll be on the march again,
Pershing led the Yanks before heading for Berlin
In every conquered land,
The folks have waited and prayed
Millions of men, with a song in their heart,
Will join the big parade.

The Dutch, Poles, Greeks, Norwegians, and the Czechs
Will soon be swarming around Berlin,
And ringing some Nazis necks.
They'll hunt out everyone and chase him down the road
And when he hollers 'camange'
We'll give him the other load.

On WWII

It's just a matter of time 'till Hitler is bound to learn,
The dream he had about ruling
The world isn't gonna work worth a durn.
And all the things he's done are coming home to roost,
'Cause millions of men are on the trail, fixin' to cook his goose.

Who does he think he is, this guy with a flat mustache?
The world was made for decent folk, not his kind of trash.
Just like his pal in Rome some day, he'll swell up and burst
And we'll hang his hide on a hickory limb,
If the Russians don't get him first.

WARS END

It's just a matter of time 'till the boys will be come marching home
After they're through with the housecleaning job in Japan, Berlin, and Rome,
Then what are we gonna do to let somebody start again
Building up their war machines, to murder millions of men
We can't go on this way with a war every 20 years.
This world was made for something else besides blood, and toil and tears

We say it can't be helped but it could
If we were smart
If we're strong enough to win these wars,
Let's stop them before they start.

MISSISSIPPI VALLEY BLUES

Many years have gone by since I wandered
From my loved ones and all that was dear to me
From my home in the Mississippi Valley
That dear old place I long to be.

Mississippi Valley I am longing for you
My poor heart is breaking
I'm sad and I'm blue.
Just to see your waters gleaming,
Of you each night I'm dreaming.
I've got the Mississippi Valley blues.

I could see my childhood chums as they wandered
Up and down the shady lanes,
Where I used to roam
I can see my dear old gray haired mother
Knelt in prayer besides the old hearthstone.

I'll go back to the Mississippi Valley,
There I'll settle down
And spend my reclining days
With my mother who is waiting and longing
For her wayward boy
Who has gone astray.

I'LL GET ALONG SOMEHOW.

Many months have come and gone,
Since you called me on the phone
To tell me that we were through,
You thought it would break my heart,
But I fooled you from the start,
'Cause I never did trust you.

You thought you were mighty wise,
To run around with other guys
And still say you were mine.
While you had one or two,
I had a dozen more than you.
So you got the foolin' that time.

Oh, let it rain or let it snow.
I don't care
Oh, no no no.

I'll never worry now,
You're the one that was unfair,
Twasn't in you to play square.
I'll get along somehow.

So you keep going your way,
I'll keep goin' mine,
But at the end,
When you'll need a friend,
You'll be the one to sit and pine.

So let it rain or let it snow.
I don't care,
Oh, no no no.
I'll get along somehow.

DON'T TELL ME ABOUT MEN

Don't talk to me about men,
Just fill my glass up again.

I want to forget every man that I met,
And the trouble they got me in.

Don't mention love to me,
I know the game A to Z,
I've carried the torch
Until there's just a scorch
In the place where my head ought to be.

They'll make your affair just a graft,
And promise they'll love you for life.
And the next thing you know,
They're gone with the draft,
Or else they show up with a wife.

So don't talk to me about men
Just fill my glass up again

I want to forget every man that I met,
And the trouble they got me in

You may be thinking I'm high as a kite,
And that I'm just acting the blues
But I've got their number,
And I've got it right,
And I didn't learn it in school.

WINKIN' AT ME

Kind friends, your attention I'll ask for a while
I'll try to amuse you in my simple style
With singin' and playin'
I'm sure it must be
But how can I sing
When they're winkin' at me?

A winkin' at me,
A winkin' at me,
How can I sing
When they're winkin' at me?

Out here sits a young man,
Dressed up in good taste.
Aside of that girl with his arm 'round her waste
A false-hearted fellow
While he makes love to her,
He keeps winkin' at me.

Down here sits a married man,
He ought to be home
A choppin' stove wood for his wife
And his own
No wonder you blush,
Married man that you be
While you sit by your wife,
You keep winkin' at me.

Out here sits a young man,
Is he getting red?
I happen to know
He's engaged to be wed.

He's holding the hand of his pal's girl I see
And to top it all off,
He keeps winkin' at me.

Now I'm not so pretty,
I very well know,
To cause all these men gawkin' so.

My shoes and my ruffles
It surely must be,
For they all take one look
And start winkin' at me.

GRACE LARSON

JUST TELL THEM THAT YOU SAW ME

While strolling down the street one eve,
Upon mere pleasure bent,
'Twas often business worries of the day
I saw a girl who shrank from me.
Of whom I recognized,
A schoolmate of a village far away
"Is that you Madge?" I said to her
She quickly turned away,
"Don't turn away Madge, for I am still your friend
Next week I'm going back to see the old folks,
And I thought some message you would like to send"

"Just tell them that you saw me,"
She said, "They'll know the rest
Just tell them I was looking well,
You know, just whisper if you get a chance,
To mother dear and say, "I love you as I did long years ago.""

Your cheeks are pale,
Your face is thin,
Come tell me you were ill,
When last we met
Your eyes shone clear and bright

Come home with me, when I go Madge,
The change will do you good
Your mother wonders where you are tonight

"I long to see them all again,
But not just yet," she said.
'Tis pride alone that's keeping me away
Just tell them not to worry,
For I'm alright, don't you know?
Tell mother; I'm coming home some day.

"My Mother"

Mom's brothers worked on the railroad, and I remember Mom mentioning Idaho Falls and Pocatello as their location at the time. When Mom and Aunt Maud came to this country, they homesteaded at Raidersburg. I believe a brother, maybe John, also homesteaded there. Mom worked at the Roundhouse in Logan.

Aunt Maud came to the ranch when we were kids. She was married to a Rude, and a Ranger. I remember the younger kids were named Mary and Bob Ranger, and the oldest was Orville Rude. Orville still lived in Laurel as far as I know; he died in the early 1990's. Mary was "Mary Wright," and lived around Harlowton on a ranch, but I haven't heard from her in years. There also was a Florence Ranger, another cousin.

Aunt Jessie lived in Washington, at Everett. Aunt Mollie was at Four Lakes, Washington. Bill and I visited her once, years ago, when we took horses to Spokane. She was at the ranch once about that time too, maybe early 1950's. Her husband's name was Bill Cudney. She died several years ago and left a trunk full of memorabilia that nobody was able to find.

I hear one of Uncle Louis's girls, Jessie Oakes, now and then. They're in Everett, Washington. Another girl, Louise, lived in Kalispell. Her son has Marilyn's Gun Shop.

Edith Killgore, #215 of Junction City, Oregon, writes:

"I am your Aunt Minnie's daughter. There were 10 of us children, 9 living, 3 boys and 7 girls. We lost our youngest brother, Archie, in Second World War. Frank & Kenneth are both Ministers of the Gospel. Frank is in Idaho, I in Oregon, Kenneth in Texas, 3 sisters in Oklahoma, 1 in Alabama and 1 in California.

"We lost Mother in 1968 and Dad in October 1970. We plan on trying to get together every 2 years. As for myself, I was left a widow in 1939. We had 6 small children. I lost my oldest daughter before my husband.

"They are all married, have large families. They all live here in Oregon except one daughter, who lives in California. I have 32 grandchildren and 6 great grandchildren. One of my sons is a minister."

Francis DesChamps was born in Paris, France, came to America in 1723. He was known as a French Huguenot. They fled because of persecution. He had 2 sons, Joseph and Peter.

Peter married Elizabeth Simmons. Had one son named Francis, our mother's great, great grandfather. He married Susanna Joy and had 3 sons: Francis, who died young, Louis, and George Sinclair Capers, and our mothers' great grandfather.

He married Elizabeth Wayne (she was related to Mad Anthony Wayne). Her mother was Esther Trezevant. They had 3 sons, Avant, William and Sinclair Capers (Capers is a family name).

Frances DesChamps was once the owner of one of the largest plantations in South Carolina.

The first Methodist Church service was held in Georgetown, South Carolina, in the home of Louis Miles DesChamps, by Bishop Francis Ashbury. Grandpa DesChamps was married in 1856 and died in 1894.

Grandma's name was Holloman. She had brothers, J.C. Garfield, and Flurry. Sisters Ada Doyle and Elizabeth Ratchford.

My mother found her grandfather's grave by the help of an old man who remembered him being shot. She did not find her father's grave.

This coincides with things that Mom told me, except for a couple of things; Edith said the 1/2 Cherokee woman's name was Mary Sims Seymour, and Mom said it was Mary Sidney Bethune Seymour.

Mom also called her great grandfather, Miles DesChamps, rather than Louis Miles.

She mentioned Grandpa DesChamps, but never could recall his first name; said that he had been shot in the pulpit. The man who shot him was named Henley, and his reason for shooting was a recent disturbance. Someone reported the man to the sheriff, and he swore to kill whoever it was. The man who reported him, Old Man Bowerman, was afraid to admit it, and said "Brother DesChamps did it." Nothing was done about it. Henley's mother was said to have gone insane over the shock. She lived alone near Poteau Mountain. She was living there when Mom was little.

Mom said Grandpa DesChamps was first a Methodist minister, and then a Missionary Baptist.

History said Pocahontas had one child, Mom said her grandma told her she had two, a boy and a girl. She was supposed to be related to Mom's grandmother.

From Grace Larson, February 1968, regarding letters to her from her grandmother, Mae Poloson (Annie Mae DesChamps):

Dated April 7, 1965, **Grandma Mae wrote:**

My sister that I haven't seen for over 45 years wrote that a cousin of ours (I don't know any of our cousins) said that she had had the DesChamps family traced back to Paris, and Mama said the members of the family that came to South Carolina left France because of religious persecution. The only name of the family at that time that I know is Colonel Miles DesChamps. That name Miles puzzles me, as it doesn't look or sound French. I wonder if it might be short for Camille which is French, but he might have been nicknamed Miles by the people of South Carolina. If you have a large encyclopedia look up the Huguenots. Mine is just one volume but it says when they had to leave France most of them settled in South Carolina and New York.

Miles DesChamps settled in South Carolina. The name was originally des Champs (of fields) meaning that the one carrying the name, or his family, was the owner of fields or a large estate.

We learned that from a French woman at Three Forks, Montana, years ago.

I'm trying to write about our people. I find I can't remember hearing my grandpa DesChamps' first name. My memory is not very good now, so I may remember it if I bump my head just right and jar my memory! The queer thing about it is I can easily remember my great grandfather's name, Miles DesChamps, but my grandpa was just called Grandpa DesChamps. He was shot in the chair behind the pulpit of his church. The pulpit is, or was, the place where the preacher delivered the sermon. He had arrived early at the church and was reading his Bible when a man named Henley walked up the aisle and shot him, and because my grandpa sat there instead of falling, this tough guy used his gun to shove him to the floor.

People just sat there, probably too scared and surprised to move, while enough (they were called desperadoes in those days) turned and walked out. Of course there was nothing they could have done, as people usually don't take guns to church.

Later it was learned that the tough guy had caused a disturbance at a baptizing, a religious rite practiced by the Baptists and some other churches, and grandpa asked for a song as it was part of the service. Before the congregation could start singing (of course he meant a sacred song) but this tough guy had had a few drinks and he started to sing "The old gray horse came a-tearin' out of the wilderness." Of course the people were shocked and angry and one hot-headed deacon reported Henley to the sheriff, for disturbing the peace at a religious gathering. The deacon got scared when the tough guy asked him if he was the man who reported him to the sheriff. The man (Mama called him old Man Bowerman) said, "No, no, it was Brother DesChamps who reported you." The tough guy said, "I promised to kill the man who reported me!"

So because Bowerman was a coward and Henley probably was drinking, he walked into the church and shot my grandfather. As far as we knew, or as Mama remembered and told us, not much was done to try to catch the murderer. By the time people got over the shock he had hid out. Henley's mother went insane from the shock. She lived alone near what was called Poteau Mountain. I don't know when she died, but she was living there when I was little.

I suppose neighbors helped her, but I don't really know. When you are young, I guess you don't question the How? or Why? of things, but if someone tells you of the "good old days," bet him a dollar he wouldn't like them if he could go back. I was born pretty near to the good old days, and as far as I'm concerned you can cross out the good. I'd rather take my chances with the uncertain new days.

My hand is tired but I'll leave my writing things here to remind me to start trying to write what I can remember of the family.

Love to all,
Grandma

Dated April 8, 1965

It might help getting information on my Grandpa DesChamps if you looked for information on the early traveling preachers. He was first a Methodist minister, and then he decided the Missionary Baptist belief was more in line with his beliefs. His wife, my father's mother, was part Virginia Cherokee Indian and claimed to be an ancestor of Pocahontas. I don't tell people she was an ancestor of my father's mother because I have no way of proving it. I'd be glad to claim her as an ancestor if I could trace my ancestors that far back. History says she had one child. My grandma told her she had two, one boy and one girl. I believe my Grandma because she had no reason for claiming it if it was not true.

My Grandma's name was Mary Sidney Bethune Seymour. I don't know the why of the Sidney, but the Bethune is not a family name, just the name of the family's favorite minister.

(Later)

Fay brought some livestock magazines and one of them from Tulsa, Oklahoma has an ad for Angus cattle for sale by Wibur J. Holleman. He almost has to be a member of my mother's family. She had a brother Flurry or Flurrey, I forget just how it was spelled, and he was there the last time we heard from him. Wilbur J. might be a great grandson of Flurry. There are also some Holleman's in Texas that are probably descendants of her brother Isom.

He used to live in Texas after he moved from Oklahoma but the part of Oklahoma where Mama's family lived was called Indian

Territory, but the Indians there were known as the Five Civilized Tribes, and they lived up to their name.

My father's parents, Grandpa DesChamps (I still can't remember any name except my grandfather's surname) and Grandma Mary Sidney Bethune Seymour. My father's name, Sinclair Capers DesChamps. My mother's father Samuel Holleman. My mother's mother, Mary Ann Douglas. Her father was John Douglas from Scotland, a member of the Douglas Clan, I suppose, as he was real Scotch including his accent in talking, Mama said. I think the Scotch use Ian for John. I don't know anything about my Grandpa Holleman's people. He came from Illinois to Missouri. I suppose he met my Grandma in Missouri, at least the Holleman children except my youngest uncle, Garfield, were born in Missouri, I think. Grandpa's records of his service in the Union Army through the Civil War are probably on file in Washington, D.C.. He had an honorable discharge and an army pension.

I don't know how my father happened to be named Sinclair Capers. It might have been family names. There is a Capers River in one of the southeastern states, so it might be it got its name from someone, but I can't find it on any maps I have now. I just remembered it because it had my father's second name and I wondered if the river was named after one of my father's relations.

I've just remembered my Grandpa Holleman had a sister named May Holleman. If records in Illinois or Missouri, or even Arkansas, may have those two names in one family, it is almost sure to be our family. May Holleman was my mother's aunt. I got my name from her. Somewhere along the way my brother started addressing his letters to "Mae," since that was the new way to spell it about the time I grew up.

Mae's Grandfather's History:

DesChamps

Louis Miles DesChamps, born: 23 Aug. 1789, Berkley District

Louis Miles Deschamps and Margaret DuBose were married 5 November 1812 - No children.

Louis Miles DesChamps married Elizabeth Trezavant Elliott 20 February 1817. (Elizabeth married first, Francis Elliott and had one Son, John Abraham Elliott, born 19 November 1810 at the time of her marriage to Louis Miles Des Champs.)

Children:
Susannah Esther DesChamps born 5 Jan. 1818
William Francis DesChamps born 26 Sept. 1819
Mary Axon DesChamps born 28 Feb. 1824
Sinclair Capers DesChamps born 23 Jan. 1826 (Mae's Grandfather)
Louis Henery DesChamps born 23 July 1830

Elizabeth Trazavant was the daughter of William and Esther Trezevant. William Wayne was the son of "Mad Anthony Wayne's" cousin both having been raised in the same home. Her mother was a Trezevant of South Carolina and may be found in the Trezavent history.

Sinclair Capers DesChamps 2nd, born 23 Jan. 1826 married Mary Seymour C.B. Sims 21 Oct. 1846

Children;
Sinclair Capers DesChamps (Mae's father)
William DesChamps
Avant DesChamps
Elizabeth DesChamps

Sinclair Capers DesChamps 2nd, Married Mary Emaline Holleman 23 July 1776.

Children:
Mary Jane born 1877
Sam Sidney born 5 July 1878

Louis Henery born 6 February 1883
Minnie Elizabeth born 1884
John William born 4 February 1887
Annie Mae born 2 February 1889
Ada Maude Born 18 February 1891
Jessie George born 8 May 1894
Two children died young, James and Capers.
My mother was Ada Maude DesChamps.

September 24, 1988
ORVILLE C. RUDE

Mae's sister

**A letter from Aunt Molly to Oriville Rude;
dated March 26, 1944
    Spokane, Washington.**

Your mother Maude has lived with a broken heart for so long now. She sits there all alone with you children gone. Orville, please go to see her as often as you can and take your wife and babies to see her.

    You asked me about your fathers' disappearance, Orville. Not much that I can tell you. He disappeared from Three Forks, Montana as completely as if the ground opened up and swallowed him. No trace at all. He was well liked by all, never talked very much. He was so good and kind to all of us. He received some money from his father's estate. Then he got a letter from someone who had hunted and trapped with in the Little Belt Mountains telling him of some homestead land. He got your grandmother, Emaline DesChamps, to come in and stay with your mother. He put your mothers' horse and wagon in the Livery Barn, paid a week's feed bill. He then got a load of wood and split it and put wood in the house, it was very cold. He came to see me and said, "Mollie, help Maude to look after my boy until I get back. I will write each day to Maude and I will be back in a week." I asked him, "Why go now? The weather is so bad." He said, "It is just right if the land is where I think it is. I know every trail there and this snow is fine to skid my logs right down to where I want them."

Your mother, Maude, never heard from him, so she was worried. We told her to wait, the weather was so bad she would hear soon. One night, she wakened her mother, crying so hard. She could not stop her. Maude finally said, "I will never see Clint again. I saw him go down in the middle of a glade in snow and ice, it covered him up, I was not asleep at all, I could not sleep!"

We had to fight her for reason one time we thought we had lost her but it was you that saved her.

I went to the city policeman (he liked Maude, always said there was no man good enough for her). I told him about not hearing from Clint. He swore vengeance on Clint, said, "If I find him and he is not hurt or sick, he will be when I find him (he knew Clint well). No one can treat Maude like that." Then I got the shock of my life when he never took the train out of Three Forks. Then we advertised, the Sheriff had his picture published and notified his mother. His mother notified his brother in Canada, I think he was a captain in the Canadian Army, or an officer of some rank. With all of the search there was no trace of Clint. The train that he intended to take was late, he came back from the Depot and left his telescopic grip at Eck and Andersons Saloon and said he "was going to White Sulphur Springs to see some Negros hanged." Well the Negros were hung but he never took that train either. Harry Rector was the Depot Agent and he knew Clint. I don't think he ever left Three Forks, I think he was murdered.

I made several trips to view dead men that were found in different places.

Further more he intended to come back to Maude for he left his mothers photo and his brothers photo, if he had been leaving for good he would have taken them with him. He disappeared just before the registration for World War One, so the Sheriff said if he is alive he will have to register and if he does, even under an assumed name, we will find him with his photo and the scars he has on his body.

Clint, Harry Gray, and Henery Webber came to Three Forks together. Henery Gray and Harry Webber said if they could get any trace of him they would let me know. I saw Harry Gray 5 years afterwards, he said he had been over a lot of country that he and Clint had worked and trapped in but no one had heard of him.

Well Orville, I hope you can read this and that you and your wife can visit us this summer.

Orville your mother cannot talk about this, about Clint. She never loved anyone like she loved him; it runs in our family to only love once. We may marry more than once. I believe that your Father loved your mother and he was the fondest father I ever saw when you arrived. When you arrived, he always did every thing to help Maude care and look after you, he was cooking and washing and any thing he could do to help Maude. He wanted her to rest so that you could grow big.

Well, bye, bye, write often, I get lonesome here. With love to all,

Your Aunt Mollie and Billie Cudney.

A Letter from Mae Poloson to her nephew Orville Rude, Dated December 28, 1960.

"Parson DesChamps," Parson is old fashioned for Preacher, who was first a Methodist minister, later changed to Missionary Baptist Church.

He had three sons, my father Sinclair (pronounced Sinkler) Capers, Avant and William. Grand Pa was a carriage maker and exempt from the draft in the Civil War, 1861-1864.

William and Avant (called Vant) were blacksmiths, but father was better at shop work than his two brothers. He was a good blacksmith and also a wagon maker. Your uncle, my brother Sam DesChamps wrote us after we came to Montana (1910) and told us he had just seen a wagon, owned by one of his neighbors, that our father had built 40-years beforehand and it was still in good useable shape. I think that shows he was good at his job.

Avant, Oklahoma was named for uncle Avant so my sister "Mollie" told me. Oklahomians accent the first "A", the French accent the last syllable I think.

Grandma was a mid-wife and a pretty good Doctor. She called herself an "Indian Doctor" but she knew a great deal about White Mans' Medicine too and called them by their Latin names. She travelled through the hills day or night when her neighbors were sick.

Her name was Mary Sidney Bethune Seymoure (or Seymour). I supposed the names Mary and Sidney were family names. Bethune was the name of the Minister of the family's Church, Seymour is English, maybe Virginians as Grandma's people came from there, though her home was Charleston, South Carolina. My father was born in South Carolina. It think he was born in Charleston, though I am not sure.

Later Grandma and Grandpa went to Louisiana, then to Texas, then to Arkansas. They traveled from Texas to Arkansas by Ox team and Grandma said as they traveled the dry Texas country the Oxen got so thirsty, they smelled water there was no stopping them, then they started to gallop and could not be stopped till they reached the creek or river. When I think of riding behind a galloping Ox-team I feel awfully guilty when I complain about how rough the country road are.

My Cherokee Grandma DesChamps smoked a pipe and probably grew her own tobacco. I suppose she started smoking on account of the long trips when she rode so far without eating and maybe smoking helped her to keep going without being so tired and hungry.

In addition to her three sons, Sinclair, Avant, and William, she had two daughters, named Sheba and Trisvan (called Trizzie) but since their families did not bear the DesChamps name, they would not be of any help in tracing the DesChamps name.

Mae's mother was named Mary Emaline Holleman, daughter of Samuel Holleman and Mary Ann Douglass Holleman, daughter of John Douglass who came from Scotland, Mary Ann Douglass was Scotch-Irish and Dutch, Mama said. I do not know if it was Holland/Dutch or Pennsylvania Dutch but I think it was Holland/Dutch. Mary Ann's father was named John Douglass ("I an" in Gallec, the old language. I have never figured out what, "I an" meant, something no doubt.) He was born in Scotland but I have not figured out if that makes us decedents of the Douglass Clan, or if there was another Douglass family in Scotland. I'd like to know. We used to read of the "Douglass in His Hall" in a poem *Marion and Douglass* by Sir Walter Scott.

I never knew much about my Grandfather Holleman. He came from Illinois to Missouri and then to Arkansas. Mae's grandmother could talk about the building of the Union Railroad (Union Pacific Railroad built through Missouri and Nebraska). She was a little girl and the railroad came through near where her family was living. She said those Irish Laborers would work hard all day and come close to fighting just as hard all night. When they got a little further west, I guess the bosses were glad they were tough. There was lots of Indian trouble, Zane Grey wrote of it in "The U.P. Trail" I think the name is.

He and my mother agreed on most of the story if not all.

Mae's Grandmother Holleman had to stay home alone while Samuel, her husband, was in the Union Army (1861-1865). Her children were John, Emmaline, Isom, and Jim at that time. Later there were others; Lizzie, Harmon, George, Clemmie, Flurry, Ada, and Garfield. I don't know if I have them down in the right order. I never saw grandma Holleman, she died when the youngest son, Garfield was born. Garfield was in the army in the Philippines after the Spanish American War. He also served in the U.S. Army during World War One. He died just about the beginning of World War Two. Otherwise, I suppose, he would have been in it too, but I think he was too old.

Grandma Holleman, during the Civil War had to do the farm work and work in the home as well. She had a shotgun but I don't know if she ever fired it. One time she took it and told a man living nearby to get his cows off her place and quit taking her fence down. He got them out without her having to use the gun.

During the War, when most of the men were away in the army, there were bands of outlaws called "bushwackers." They roamed the woods robbing old men and lone women. They made a special effort to get the money the soldiers' wives drew for support of their families.

Three of them came to Grandma Holleman's home and started to threaten her because she refused to tell them where her ration money was. They did not hurt her but the leader kept talking rougher and Grandma got mad. She went to the fireplace and grabbed a chunk of pine, a blazing chunk of pitch pine and swung it at him. She set his cook skin cap on fire and it bled up the tail and on up to the top of his head. He ran outside and saw his men laughing at him so I guess he thought they wouldn't want him to get rough with a woman like Grandma.

The money was still safe. One of the small boys sat on a piece of log because they did not have enough chairs. Grandma had bored a hole in the bottom of the block, put her money in the hole and stuffed cotton in it to keep the money from falling out. That is the only time I can remember Mama saying anything about any trouble at home while Grandpa Holleman was in the army.

I remember Grandfather Holleman was always glad to see him when he came to visit me.

Mae DesChamps Poloson

To those who read this letter; Aunt Mae's Father died when she was very young. She was raised by her mother and older brothers and sisters. Family history as she knows it was told to her by these people. Little family recorded history was ever saved.

Orville C. Rude

From Mae's cousin Elizabeth Johnson, Our Cherokee doctor Grandmother's pipe smoking

About the pipe smoking;

It wasn't tobacco according to all of the relatives here. It was a combination of herbs and weeds, including Jimson Weed, which she used for treating her asthma as well as my great grandmother's. In 1960, I took my mother to find the cemetery. We went to Stella DesChamps home. She was the last wife of Sam DesChamps. (I think he had three or four...) Stella had known Mary, our great, great grandmother, Sinclair Capers DesChamps' (1) wife. She commented on Mary DesChamps height and said that she was very dark. I've been told by quite a few people that she was near 6 feet tall, which I believe for no other reason than my grandmother's height. She was 5 ft. 11 inches as were both of her sisters. We went to Buggy Hill Cemetery and also to the home of a very old gentleman who was about 8 years old when Sinclair Capers DesChamps was killed. He lived just down the road from Sinclair C. DesChamps (1)' home. He went to his funeral with his father and to the graveyard. There is no gravestone but he was able to tell us exactly where the grave was (the number of steps from the corner of the grave with the five sets of twins) by the "oak tree." He said that S.C. DesChamps was shot while sitting on his front porch. My grandmother had said that Sinclair Capers DesChamps was shot in his pulpit.

EPILOGUE

Fay has moved into extended Care, St Lukes, in Ronan. A fall in late February 2019 landed her in the hospital, and for several weeks the doctors thought she might not make it. But Fay has the same determination now that she had as a young girl. Fay enjoys visits from her friends and TJ, the Miniature Australian Shepherd, who made his home with her for over six years.

As I am putting this book, FAY, together, I am grateful for her wonderful memory.

Questions come up and, for the most part, Fay can answer them.

Fay Poloson Haynes Obituary

RONAN — Fay Poloson Haynes was born January 4, 1926 in Helena, Montana. Fay's mother, Annie Mae DesChamps Poloson, was born in Indian territory, Mansfield, Arkansas, Feb. 8, 1889. Mae came west by train in 1910 and homesteaded near Three Forks, Montana.

Fay's father, Dan Poloson, was born Oct. 26, 1896 near Porumbacu, Romania. Dan immigrated to the United States in 1916. He was working for the Herron Sheep Ranch near Wolf Creek when he and Mae were married March 2, 1922.

They bought the Rattlesnake Gulch Ranch in 1929. Fay was three years old when they moved, by train, from Wolf Creek, Montana to the Lonepine-Niarada area ranch.

Fay went to school at Lonepine, Montana.

Fay was a woman of so many talents. She could sew beautifully, making most of her and Bill's shirts, dress coats, and dress slacks.

Embroidery and, even crewel, were skills she developed. It took her almost two years to complete the crewel of Bill on horseback. Fay's oil and pencil paintings are so well defined. She could make "melt in your mouth" pie crust too.

Fay knew good horses and rode many of them. Her very favorites were Pal and Night, and next was Jule Bar. Jule Bar and his son, Jumpy Jule took Fay all the way to the Montana Cowboy Hall of Fame. She won so many barrel racing, pole bending, and western show events over the years. She performed at the Calgary Stampede, Walla Walla and Grand Coulee, Washington, Lethbridge, Canada, and in most of Montana's rodeos.

Fay's rodeo life began when she was a teenager. She was chosen rodeo queen and held that title for several years at the Polson, Hot Springs, and Plains, Montana rodeos.

She was secretary for Jake Johnson's rodeo events for close to 10 years. Fay knew rodeo stock and met many good cowboys over the years.

The cowboy she fell in love with was working as a judge at the Polson rodeo. He had a wrist injury, so he wasn't riding bulls, bareback horses, or bulldogging. Fay and he started talking and ended up married Dec. 15, 1951.

They bought the Big Bend Ranch from Bud Lake and began their life of raising top quality horses and prize Angus cattle.

Fay is preceded in death by her husband Bill Haynes, her parents, brothers Fred and Bert, sister Marie, sisters-in-law Grace, Betty and Ann, niece Robin and nephew Dan. Fay is survived by nephew Russell Poloson, nieces Jeanne Poloson Bronec, Alice Kranzler, Grace Larson and Shirley Jacobsen, and by so many who considered her friend, aunt, grandmother.

Funeral services will be held at 10 a.m. on Saturday, Nov. 30 at the Ronan Community Center. Interment will follow at Murray Memorial Cemetery in Lonepine, Montana.

Fay and Lucille Roullier in the old convertible on their way to the Calgary Stampede in 1945.

Fay & TJ September 2019

www.ingramcontent.com/pod-product-compliance
Ingram Content Group UK Ltd.
Pitfield, Milton Keynes, MK11 3LW, UK
UKHW022228230426
12048UKWH00016BA/1137